I0704107

Speak Softly, and Carry a Gavel

Written by

Hoob Jorgenbergenmussen

<u>Dedicated to</u>

Steve Preston

Yes I'm selfish! Seeing You Happy?

All About Me!

Love Ya' Brother!

Chapter 1

A World, a Country, or View can change in the blink of an eye, with either the rise, or fall, of any scenario where even One is affected. In the summer of 2022, the Supreme Court of the United States of America, overturned one of the most vital 'Laws of Reproductive' decision making, taking the value, and idea of choice, from the families, and individuals, away, and placing that choice in the hands of the States and Government. As the Administrations came, and went, that 'Change' still haunted the People, and their Representatives, until it had a Voice that could really give Change, the Justice it deserved.

The television cameras zoomed in on Leticia as she waved to the few that stood outside the small bar in Northern California, agents in Yellow surrounding her at a few arms-length, but still close enough to protect her if needed. The News Stations and Anchors had just proclaimed Leticia Gonzalez had won her re-election, and the moment she heard the words of her success, she uttered the three words, "Take the shot" into the phone that would alter her next four years, and beyond.

'THWUP!', 'PPSCCHEW', came two sounds from two large-caliber rifles. The first round, streaking through the air, as the sun lit its way towards its unsuspecting victim. The second round, silently swirling through the night, the moon secretly guiding the projectile towards its celebrating target.

'THUD!'.

'CRACK!'.

One round hit its mark.

The other stopped by protective-glass.

And Leticia stood there, smiling, and waving as if nothing had happened.

Chapter 2

The morning after the election, while sitting in her Hotel room on the coast of Northern California, Leticia's cellphone rang on the table next to her plate of scrambled-eggs, a large mound of bacon, two-slices of toast, and a half of a grapefruit. Looking at the caller-ID, Leticia smiled, as she pressed the 'Answer' button, and pressed the 'speaker-phone' button, "Good morning, Holly.." she said gleefully as she picked up a piece of bacon, and took a large bite, chewing slow to savor the bacon's greasy flavors.

"It's a morning, alright" Holly replied over the phone, her voice not exactly pleasant, "Did you get the report from last night?" she asked, her tone quite irritated.

Leticia looked at her small table, and saw the folder across from her, "Yeah, it's right here" she said, stuffing the rest of the bacon strip in her mouth as she reached for the folder, pulling the papers from it, and beginning to read as she chewed, and picked up a piece of toast, "What the fuck?" she said quickly, putting down the toast, "Who shot at you?" she asked, continuing to read.

Holly took a few deep breaths and chuckled, "Oh, they found the guy.." she said with a tone of sarcasm, "turns out to be a woman.." she said, and paused.

Leticia looked up from her papers, her eyes wide and her mouth opened in shock.

"So, we will be landing at the airfield up there in about four hours" Holly said matter-of-factly into the phone, "and have a little, umm, Re-election Celebration!" she said with a hint of mystery.

Leticia shook her head and closed her mouth at the idea, giving a slight chuckle as she too was interrupted, and handed another file, "Hold on one sec, Holly" she said as she took the second folder and placed it on the first, pulling the papers from it, reading quietly for a moment, and smiling, "Well, it will be quite the celebration then my friend" she said with a tone of excitement, "We have two up here as well, that were caught sneaking into a fire-evacuation zone, man and woman.." she said as she read, "and the two fuckers were caught with a car full of stolen shit.." she said with excitement in her voice.

"What?" Holly replied.

Leticia laughed as she read, "Drugs, paraphernalia, watches, money, clothes.." she listed as she shook her head.

"Well, Boss.." Holly said, her voice soft, "no matter how much we do, or how much you give back.." she said with compassion and support, "there are some that don't know how to be members of society, and only want to inflict pain on those who work hard" she said sadly.

Leticia agreed as she nodded, still reading the report she was handed, "I'm glad your safe, Holly" she said, shaking her head as she pushed the papers away from her, as she looked at her breakfast plate, picking up a piece of bacon, and looked at it, "You have an idea on how to make an example of these three?" she asked, taking a bite of the fatty-goodness, and looking at her phone for the reply.

The line was quiet for a moment, "I've got an 'Ace' up my sleeve for something neat" she replied with a chuckle, "See you about noon, Madam President.." she said professionally, "And, congratulations on your re-election" she said, and paused.

Leticia smiled and nodded, chewed and swallowed, "Thank you, Holly, see you soon" she said, pressing the 'end-call' button on her phone, smiling at her mound of bacon, reaching for the television remote, pressing the power button, and waiting for the News to come on so she could hear about all the reports from the Election process from the night before.

At noon precisely, a large helicopter landed at the small airport in Northern California, as Holly disembarked the large compartment through the side door, walking down the metal steps, and towards a 1948 Black Ford truck with Red trim, shiny wheels, and a .50cal gun-mount in the bed, with an agent in Yellow at the ready, strapped in with support straps. Holly got in the passenger-side of the guarded vehicle, buckled her seatbelt, and waited for her Yellow Fedora'd driver to take her to her destination.

The local Courthouse had no yard, or lawn, just a small parking-lot that had been closed off and emptied, with a large stage erected, and cover with a large, black-cloth covering that gently swayed in the Fall-breeze in front of the sliding-glass doors, facing the street. Several video crews from the big stations showed, and waited, as the President took her place at the podium to the right of the stage, with Holly to her right, and an agent in a Red Fedora to her left, holding a compound-bow in one hand, and a carbon-fiber arrow with a unique tip in the other.

Leticia stood at the small podium next to the covered-stage, and smiled to the crowd as it filled the closed-off parking lot, "Good morning!" she erupted, throwing her hands in the air as she stood there smiling in her Brown suit, hair pulled back, her face lightly covered in makeup, "Today, marks a special day for the People and Residents of this beautiful, and majestic, Northern California town, here in Crested Cove" she said nodding to those around her, "It has been an honor, and blessing, to call Gasquet a home for the last few days, and making her a favorite destination when time allows" she smiled and nodded to the cameras and locals.

The camera panned from Leticia, to the crowd, back to the President, and wide-angled back to fit the Leader and stage in the screen.

Leticia nodded and gripped the sides of the podium, "Your County has been plagued by such inept corruption, at its highest level" she said sternly to those in attendance, "that allows the scum of your streets, to wander free, rather than upholding the Laws and Reforms the state handed down seven-years ago" she said, looking to her left at the agent, and the covered stage, raising her hand slightly to give a signal, and suddenly, the black-covering fell, revealing five individuals, lined up facing the agent in the Red Fedora and President.

The five we lined up, hands bound and raised above them, their heads secured straight and lined up perfectly with each other, their eyes forced open with duct-tape, and their mouths forced open with mouth-gags used in extreme-adult movies of gagging or worse, and their feet bound to the floor of the stage. None could move even if they wanted too.

Leticia shook her head as she introduced the five, "The first, your inept DA!" she erupted, and heard the boo's from the crowd, "Your inept Judge!" she yelled again, and once again the boo's came, "The thieves of your beloved homes!!" she screamed and incited, as the crowd jeered and hissed, a few throwing rocks from the crowd, and Leticia looked out quickly, pointing to the crowd, "grab the ones that threw the rocks, we will deal with them after this" she said quickly and sternly, watching as several agents entered the crowd, and pulled four persons, setting them aside and being guarded.

Leticia shook her head at the crowd and its actions, "Zero-Crime People" she said, shaking her head and finger, and looked at the last person in the line on the stage, "Rebekkha Patrovichki.." she announced, grabbing the podium once more, and looking at Holly for a moment, then back to the assassin, "the Russian President's top marksman" she said with conviction as she glared at the dangling woman, her mouth gapped open as tears rolled down her face, "and a loaned assassin.." she grunted, scowling at the woman.

The crowd pumped their fists as the dark clouds above them began to gently rain, the stage beginning to moisten, as agents stepped forward with umbrellas to cover Leticia and Holly.

Leticia looked at the crowd, then the cameras, and back to the stage, "You have been tried, and found guilty.." she said quickly as the rain began to fall harder, "Agent, to the ready.." she said, reaching on the podium and picking up a gavel as the agent in the Red Fedora raised the bow and nocked the arrow, aiming it at the mouth-opening of the DA, as Leticia quickly struck the wooden block the wooden-mallet rested on.

The agent in the Red Fedora released the arrow at the sound, the metal carbon-fiber shaft and metal tip spinning quickly through the air and rain towards the first mouth, entering, and exiting quickly through the neck and severing the spinal cord, as it entered the Judge's mouth, and exited the neck, entering the female thief's mouth, exiting her neck, entering the male thief's mouth and exiting his neck, and lastly, entering the Russian's mouth, and exiting through her neck, again, severing her spinal cord. The act took less than two-seconds, as the arrow exited the last neck, and stuck in the wooden frame of the stage. The bodies fell as one, slumping as they hung by their arms that were attached by ropes to the support beam above them. Blood pooling from their mouths and necks, mixing with the rain that soaked their bodies, and pooled on the stage beneath them.

The crowd went silent. The rain falling harder on them, and yet, they were unfazed. They had just watched their first live execution, and while they had seen one on television, they were shocked. For a moment.

"Yeeaaahhhhhhhh!" the crowded cheered after a few moments, their arms and fists pumping in the air and rain as they felt the burdens leave them and their county.

Leticia smiled and nodded, as she and Holly were escorted from her podium to the Presidential vehicle, by the Agents who held the umbrellas. The two left the Courthouse, heading towards the airfield, and on their way back to Washington D.C.

"She was found with this.." Holly said as they sat in their seats on the Presidential plane, readying to take-off, and handed Leticia a small cardboard box.

Leticia looked at the box, contorted her face with confusion, and took the box from Holly.

"Seems this goes deeper than we thought" Holly said as she watched Leticia open the box.

Leticia opened the box, and was confused by the coin she saw, "A penny?" she asked, looking at the 'Indian-head penny', her brow furrowing with confusion.

Holly scoffed, exhaling loudly, "Look at the date" she said, a hint of defeat in her voice.

Leticia looked at the date on the penny, and shook her head, "1871..?" she asked rhetorically, looking up at Holly, "When the.." she began, and was cut-off quickly.

"Yes, Ma'am.." Holly nodded to agree, "when the country was sold to the highest bidder, and the people were considered property.." she said with disgust, "Legal slavery.." she added, her tone heavy with sadness.

Leticia thought for a moment about the term, 'Legal Slavery', thought back to Abe Lincoln and the Proclamation he signed, "Fucking, Uncle Larry.." she said, shaking her head, and thinking about the reasons she hated the birth, and growth, of the Country she called home.

Chapter 3

With the election over, and the country getting back to its 'Regularly Scheduled Programs', Leticia and her Staff were eagerly awaiting Thanksgiving, and the Winter holidays they enjoyed so much. Leticia knew she had other reforms, tasks, and agendas she had to get too and sign, but after her long and tiring Campaign trail, she was ready for a few days of rest, and relaxation.

The Thursday before Thanksgiving, as Leticia was sitting at her Presidential desk, spinning the '1871 penny' on her desk and watching it twirl, she was interrupted by Holly, and three agents in Purple Fedoras.

"Madam President?" Holly asked sweetly as she entered the office, walking between two agents in Yellow, "Do you, have a moment, Ma'am?" she asked as politely as she could.

Leticia had never seen Holly this way, this distraught, and gave the wide-hipped woman her full attention as the penny slowed from spinning on the wooden desk, "Holly? Please, sit.." she offered as she too stood from her desk, and walked to the heavy chair next to where she offered Holly to sit, "What's, what's going on?" she asked sympathetically.

Holly shook her head as she sat, her face contorting with pain and confusion, with a hint of shame, as she reached down to pull a file from her handbag, handing it over to Leticia, "The youth.." she said, shaking her head.

Leticia took the file, opened it, and looked at the colorful charts and graphs, "What is this?" she asked, flipping the pages and scanning the information.

Holly took a deep breath, obviously more troubled than she should be, "This, Leticia, is the future of our youth" she said with a hint of sarcasm.

Leticia looked at Holly with a raised eyebrow the moment she heard her name, and not her title, "Our what?" she asked, looking at the charts and graphs again.

Holly squeezed herself from her chair, her colorful dress swaying as she walked towards the coffee pot, "We set all these reforms in place for inmates, convicts.." she said with a wave of her hand above her, "holding people accountable, saving the tax-payers billions a year.." she said with pride, "and adding hundreds of millions into education, right?" she asked, reaching the coffee and pouring herself a cup.

Leticia set the file down, "Yeah, and the educational test scores haven't been higher" she added with a smile, "right?" she asked for confirmation.

Holly nodded in agreement, spinning and showing a forced smile, "Yes, scores for those in attendance" she said, taking a sip of her hot drink, and walking back to her seat, "You know what a 'SARB' is Ma'am?" she asked as she got to her seat, and wedged her wide and supple behind into the chair.

Leticia thought for a moment, and shook her head, "No, I don't think so" she replied.

Holly set her cup down, and leaned back in her chair, folding her hands and fingers on her chest, "When a child ditches school, or is absent for a number of days in a row, there is a meeting with the teachers, parents, and kid.." she began, her smile fading, "and when the child misses enough days, the parents are then held responsible, even though they drop their kid off, and watch them enter the school…" she said, her tone stern, "and with our research, this begins about seventh-grade.." she added, nodding to the file, "while we closed the jails and prisons, seems, we forgot a generation and age-group" she said, her eyes sadder.

Leticia picked the file back up, and began re-reading the charts and graphs. Her eyes scanning side to side, as they widened, and her mouth began to fall open, "Are, are you serious?" she asked, reaching up with her free hand to rub her brow.

Holly tilted her head, "The parents of the kids face jail time, CPS reports, fines.." she listed, shaking her head, and sitting up in her seat, "I, have a sister.." she said, and paused.

Leticia looked up instantly, her eyes fixed on the saddened eyes of her friend.

"Joan has two kids, my niece and nephew, twins.." Holly said, holding back tears, "and in the last year, my sister has been to court for her kids seven times, spent nine days in jail, and has fines in excess of nine-thousand dollars..” she said sadly, “she and her husband have lost their jobs because of this, the kids are in foster-care, and still not attending school, yet nothing, and I mean fucking nothing, happens to the foster parents for the same infractions..” she said, anger growing in her voice as she slapped the arm of the chair.

Leticia listened, shaking her head at the story, looking at the agents by the door, then back to her friend, “What can we do?” she asked, reaching out to place her hand on Holly’s arm to calm her, and show support.

Holly looked at the gesture, smirked a little, and reached into her handbag for another file, pulling it and handing it to Leticia, “This, is a proposal, Moxie and I thought of last night..” she said proudly.

Leticia took the file, pulled the small stack of paper-clipped papers, looked at the first page for a few moments, and then at Holly, “Holly..” she said with a hint of satisfaction, “this is..” she said, turning her attention back to the pages at hand.

Holly stood and began to pace, “These kids today, they think the laws don’t apply to them..” she said quickly and defensively, "they think the laws are there to protect them, but they don't have to what, obey the laws or rules until they are eighteen?" she asked, putting Leticia on the spot.

Leticia continued to read as she listened, nodding as she did both.

"These parents teach their kids right from wrong from the moment they can walk and talk, right?" Holly asked, getting the attention of her Leader, "and for the most part, they do, until that fucking age.." she said, pointing to the charts and graphs file.

Leticia looked at the other file and chuckled, looking back at Holly, "Some will say, 'kids will be kids'.." she replied, knowing the answer and statement would infuriate Holly.

Holly glared at Leticia for a moment, "Fuck 'em" she replied.

Leticia sat tall instantly at the response from Holly, her eyes widening, "What?" she replied queerly.

Holly stood firm, "You heard me, Ma'am" she said proudly, "Fuck 'em" she repeated, "They know how to act and behave, don't they?" she asked rhetorically, "read over the proposal, and give me a call when you're done" she said, walking to her chair and picking up her handbag, "It's just a reform, Madam President, for the People.." she said with a nod, looking at her agents in Purple with another nod, and leaving the office between the two seated-Agents in Yellow.

Leticia watched her friend leave the office, and looked at the files and proposal in front of her. How could she have overlooked the kids, youth, and future generations? She thought she had given them everything with the education reforms and tax-breaks, but then she remembered, that spoiling a child, rarely leads to ripe fruit. Leticia stood from her seat, took the files to her desk, sat, and began looking over them deeply.

Three hours later, Leticia picked up her phone, dialed a few numbers, and waited.

"Yes, Ma'am" Holly's voice said as she answered.

"Your Reform goes into effect Inauguration Day" Leticia said proudly, as she closed a file on her desk, and pushed it away.

"Yes, Ma'am, thank you, Ma'am" Holly replied.

"Tim and Kim will be the first to enter the Reform" Leticia replied as she reached for another file on her desk, "the 'Nulla Reditus Reform Camp', for those 'wayward teens who need a little, extra attention.." she added with a smile and sense of mystery.

A light chuckle came from the other end of the phone, "And of the Probation and Juvenile Detention Centers?" she asked, and waited.

Leticia smiled as she flipped a page on her desk, "Close them all.." she said happily, "We still have that place down near Gitmo no one knows about, we will make that the island for Nulla Reditus" she said with a chuckle.

The other end of the line was silent for a moment, "And of my sister, and brother-in-law?" she asked, and paused.

"Already taken care of" Leticia said, and hung up the phone.

Chapter 4

The first year of Leticia's second-term unfolded as she had planned, with the impending closures of the Probation and Youth Detention Centers, and the cries and complaints of the upcoming 'Youth Crime Bill Act', the President was more adamant her Country, and Administration, be the front-runner for safety amongst its streets and people. As the year ended, the Holiday's were celebrated, and the reforms took on their final phases, Leticia made her annual trip to the Northern California town of Gasquet, and her favorite bar.

The walls of the bar had been refinished with an oak-paneling, and fresh green carpet had been laid. There were new mirrors behind the bar, as well as a new register, new fridges, and the same Purple Fedora hanging above the register as a tribute to the Bartender who lost his life. Leticia sat at the bar, looked at the Fedora, and smiled as she thought about the man who wore it.

The new Bartender was a simple woman, with red hair, thick arms and legs, a round face with a missing front-tooth, and freckles across her nose and covering her cheeks. Her blue-blouse hung low in the front exposing her ample cleavage, and necklace of a Cross.

Leticia looked up at the Fedora, then at the empty seats in the bar, and at the door that was being guarded by her Agents in Yellow Fedora's, "What time y'all get busy in here?" she asked, looking up at the dry-erase boards and the list of drinks and prices.

The Bartender smiled as she dried the glasses and set them on the counter, looking in the mirror at the Leader of the Free World, "We open at Four.." she said, setting the dry glass down as she picked up another, "but I get here early to clean and shit, ya know" she said casually to the President, "Can I get you something?" she asked, setting the next glass down and turning to give her attention to the only person in the bar.

Leticia looked at the woman, then up at the list again, "Gimme one of those, 'Moheetoe's' she laughed at the misspelling of the drink.

The Bartender chuckled as she began making the drink, "The old Bartender, had quite the sense of humor" she said as she shook her head, muddling the lime and mint leaves in the shaker.

Leticia smiled at the remark, "That, he did.." she replied, "You, have kids?" she asked, trying to get to know the woman a little better.

The Bartender nodded, "Two girls, and three boys" she said with a smile.

Leticia's eyes widened, "Whoa, five huh?" she asked, sitting tall on her barstool.

The woman chuckled, "Yeah, guess I just don't know when to tell them to pull out" she laughed as she looked at the President, and caught herself, "Oh, fuck, Madam President, I am so sorry" she said, stopping her drink making=process and looking embarrassed.

Leticia laughed and waved it off, "Show me a guy that knows when and how to pull out.." she laughed encouragingly, "What's your name?" she asked, folding her hands in front of her and leaning on the bar a little.

The Bartender looked up with a smile, "Heather, but my friends call me Jugs" she laughed, looking at her cleavage, and finished making the drink, pouring it in a glass with ice, garnishes, and sliding it to Leticia, as the main doors to the Bar opened, and three men entered, "Well, looks like quiet time is over" she chuckled as the men entered, and wandered to the far end of the bar.

"How's your day, Jugs?" the oldest of the three asked as he sat in his usual spot, adjusting his old hat on his head, and looking at the new Guest at the bar, "Ma'am.." he said as he motioned with his hat a slight nod and tip.

"Gentlemen.." Leticia said as she held up her glass to the men, and smiled, "Having a good Friday so far?" she asked, taking a sip of her drink and looking at Heather, "Wow, nice job" she said with a nod, "Get those boys anything they want, on me.." she said with a wink, taking another sip.

The three men nodded and thanked Leticia, looked at each other, and then at the windows to the bar as they heard a familiar noise in the distance, "Is it four-

PM already?" one of the men asked, as the other two nodded in frustration.

Heather placed three brown bottles in front of the men, "I tried parking in their way, but we will see how that pans out" she said, looking out the window to her green car at the end of the dirt lot.

Leticia looked at the four, then over her shoulder out the window, and listened intently, "What's, what's going on?" she asked, spinning on her stool with her drink in her hand.

The noise got louder and closer, quickly.

"Well, we got these teens, who think they own it all.." the bald man said as he grabbed his beer, and took a quick sip, "speed through here, tearing up the parking lot, grass.." he said, waving his arm in angst.

Leticia listened for a moment, "Kids will be kids.." she said in a questioning tone, listening as the noise was close.

A moment later, three quads, and two dirt bikes, raced into view, using the dirt-walk way between the trees to jump their ATV's, narrowly missing the green vehicle, and landing loudly into the gravel, turning sharply to kick up rocks and create grooves in the parking lot, then racing off to their next destination.

Leticia sat dumbfounded, looked at the three men, and Heather, and looked out the windows once more, "Daily?" she asked, reaching for her drink, and looking to the door as several others entered, then back out the window to the green vehicle.

The three men and Heather nodded in unison, as Heather greeted the new patrons and took their orders. The men began conversing quietly amongst themselves, nodding and pointing, then leaving the bar to play billiards. Leticia thought for a few moments as she starred out the window, and smiled when she saw a familiar vehicle pull in, spun around on her stool, freshened herself up in the bar-mirror, and waited.

The doors opened, as Holly and Moxie entered the bar, and their demeanor was not pleasant. Holly walked towards Leticia, as Moxie held up two fingers and mouthed the word 'Tequila' to Heather, who nodded.

Holly approached Leticia, shook her head, and pulled a folder from her bag in her left hand, "VP is dead.." she said, handing the folder to her Boss, "and it gets worse.." she said as she watched Leticia set down her drink, and take the folder.

Heather slid two shots across the bar, as Moxie took them, and handed one to Holly. The women toasted quietly, took their shots, and placed the glasses on the bar as Leticia opened and read the contents.

"Are you fucking kidding me?" Leticia asked loudly, making the patrons on the bar look at her.

"No, Ma'am.." Holly replied as she held up two fingers to Heather, "He tanked them all" she said, shaking her head as she hoisted her large bottom on a stool next to Leticia.

Heather filled the glasses, and nodded as she tended to the other patrons, turning on the music to give the President and her Staff a little privacy.

Leticia read and shook her head, "How did she die?" she asked, reading the file.

Moxie stepped forward and grabbed her shot from the counter, "The report says DKA, but she wasn't Diabetic, so we are having our people look into it" she said as she rubbed a small device that was attached to her arm known as a CGM, holding up her shot slightly in respect to the fallen Leader, and drinking the contents before placing the glass on the counter, "we have a feeling she was poisoned, but then we have to ask, by who?" she said as she looked at Holly.

Leticia listened as she read, closed the file, and handed it back to Holly, "And how the fuck, did Larry tank Wall Street?" she asked, looking at Heather and holding up three fingers, "Three more of those, and a round for the bar, please" she said with a smile, then it fade as she looked at Holly and Moxie, "Our banks?" she asked, looking up at the small television in the corner and its black-screen.

Moxie pulled a stool from behind Holly, and sat, "Best we can figure, late last night, Larry decided to close nearly seventy-percent of all the stores and businesses, firing nearly every employee, and creating so much uncertainty and panic.." she began as Leticia held up her hand to stop her.

The shots arrived on the counter, and Leticia took hers quickly, drinking it, and reaching for another, "That mother fucker.." she said, taking the second, drinking it, and placing the glass next to the first empty one, then reaching for the third.

Moxie and Holly looked at each other, then at their Boss, and waited.

Leticia drank the third, "It's all fun and games.." she said as she slid the empty glass with the others, and picked up her mint-drink, rising from her stool, and walking towards the window as she looked at the green vehicle and paused, "I want a fence put up, right... there.." she said as she pointed to the trees, "all the way.. too.. there.." she said as she pointed from the trees down to where the building ended, "and add another layer of gravel to the lot, will ya'?" she asked as she smiled.

"Yes, Ma'am" Moxie said as she pulled her notepad from her pocket, and jotted down the requests.

Leticia look a long sip from her straw in her drink, the ice tinking as it hit the bottom of the empty glass, "And, set up a meeting with Larry, will you?" she asked in a casual tone, "After the Anniversary speech, of course" she said with a chuckle as she jiggle her glass in her hand, making the ice tink again, then turning around and looking at the Fedora above the bar, "and bring me the Agent in White, please.." she said, holding up her glass to Heather, and smiling, "One more round!" she erupted, swinging her arms in the air.

The few patrons in the bar cheered, as several more vehicles pulled into the parking lot, and the Friday night at the Bar began its usual night of entertainment.

The next morning, Leticia and her motorcade drove South and stopped for breakfast at a small Café. Being seated at a small table, handed a menu, the President was the new topic in the Café amongst the patrons, and she loved it. She ordered coffee, omelets for her four Agents, and waited to place her own order for a few more minutes. Her coffee was delivered to her table, and she got lost in watching a small family not far from her.

The mom was seated across from two-small boys, about nine-years old, and with obviously more energy than the mom could handle alone. A young woman approached, and sat next to the mom, and helped with one of the boys. Food was cut, drinks were played with, and all the while, the mom stayed cool and calm, and not once raised her voice. It was a setting for controlled-chaos.

Leticia watched the interaction for a few more minutes, and when the waitress approached, "So, I would like one of your large pancakes, and two scrambled eggs, six pieces of bacon, and three pieces of sausage, with marmalade, not syrup, okay?" she asked as the waitress scribbled quickly.

"Yes, Ma'am" she replied with a smile as she finished writing, and looked up as she took the menu, "Is there anything else?" she asked.

Leticia smiled as she looked at the family in the corner again, "Yes, please add her check to mine, and keep it between us, okay?" she asked nicely as she gently pointed to the mom and her small family.

The waitress smiled and nodded, "Of course" she replied as she looked at the corner, and left.

Four omelets were delivered to the two Agents at the door, and to the car. The Agents at the door held their bags, as the Agents in the car ate behind the dark-tinted glass, and then switched with the Agents at the door.

Leticia's breakfast was delivered just as the mom from the table was walking past to use the restroom, "You are doing an amazing job" she said sweetly to the mom as she walked by.

The woman was surprised, and paused, looked at Leticia, and smiled, "Well, thank you" she said, placing her hand on her chest, her face turning red, as she continued to walk towards the restrooms.

Returning to her table, the mom walked by Leticia again, and smiled, "Thank you, again" she said with a nod and sweet tone.

Leticia nodded and smiled, her mouth full of food, as she watched the mom walk back to her table. The two women ate, casually looking in each other's direction on occasion, always with a smile and nod. Leticia admired the single mom and how she raised and treated her kids, and while she thought about Holly's niece and nephew, this moment gave her hope and faith.

When the mom had finished her meal, she looked at Leticia, who had silently offered the empty seat at her small table. The mom smiled and nodded, talked to the young woman, motioned to the boys, got up from her seat, and walked to sit with Leticia.

"Madam President" the mom said as she stood at the back of the empty chair.

Leticia nodded with a soft smile as she offered the open seat, "Please" she said, "and call me Leticia, please, at least this morning" she chuckled as she took a sip of coffee.

The waitress appeared quickly, and took the empty plates from the table, making room for the women to talk.

The mom sat in the seat, set her cup down, scooted her seat in, and smiled, "How are you finding our little slice of paradise?" she asked with a soothing tone.

Leticia felt a wave of ease flow over her at the sound of the sweet voice, "I love it here" she said as she looked around, "I am thinking of buying a place up there in the Gasquet.." she said as she pointed up the road.

"That's where we live" the mom said as she sipped her coffee.

"What do you do?" Leticia asked.

The mom smiled and looked at the table with her boys, "Raise them" she said with a chuckle, "with the help of my daughter, Roo" she said as her face beamed and her smile grew.

Leticia smiled, "That's a cute name, Roo.." she said as she too looked at the table of kids, "And you? What is your name?" she asked, looking at the mom again.

The mom smiled as she turned her attention back to the President, "Me?" she asked, placing her hand on her chest, sounding and acting shy, "Sundae, Sundae Jones.." she said coyly, almost as if she was a virgin being asked to the prom.

Leticia nearly chuckled at the response, and the image of a fragile deer popped in her head.

"Hey little lady, I see you brought your boys again?" came a deep, male voice next to Sundae's daughter.

"Excuse me a sec, please?" Sundae said quickly as she set her cup down, stood as she pushed her seat out, and stormed to her table of kids, grabbing the man by his neck, squeezing her nails into his neck, and pulling her arm back to jerk his head back, "I have fucking told you, over, and over, and over.." she said in a growl as she pulled the man towards the door, with her nails in his neck, "to stay the fuck away from my daughter, you sick fuck.." she growled as she pushed the glass-door open, pulled him to the first parking spot next to the Agents car, and released him with her nails pulling from his skin as he fell to the ground, grasping his neck, "Next time, I will fucking kill you, you understand me?" she screamed as onlookers starred out the window.

Sundae smoothed her attire, nodded to the Agents with a scowled-grin, and walked back into the Café to rejoin Leticia. Pulling her chair towards her bottom as she sat, Sundae shook her head and rolled her eyes, forced a smile, and reached for her cup of coffee, "Sorry about that" she said embarrassed, "But, those kids mean everything to me" she said as she looked at her table, "And some people think they can prey on others.." she snarled through her smile as she thought about the man, turning her attention back to Leticia, and waiting.

Leticia listened and absorbed the moment, understanding the need to protect those you hold dear, as well as holding others accountable, as she looked to the door and nodded to her Agents, then looked at Sundae Jones with reverence, "How would you like to be my new VP?" she asked, picking up her cup of coffee, and holding it out for Sundae to toast.

The words hit Sundae like a train, as she was not political, and had no intention of ever running for any type of Office, but as she looked at the face of the President across from her, at the extended cup pointed at her, she thrust out her own cup, smiled, and toasted her new Boss, "Sounds, exciting!" she exclaimed as she took a sip, not exactly sure what it was she had just gotten herself into.

The two women sat at the table for another fifteen minutes, talked about a political views and affiliations, dreams and goals, made plans for Sundae and her kids to move to DC, and planned for her to be sworn in and appointed right before the Anniversary speech. They smiled, shook hands, and hugged as Sundae gathered her kids, and went home, while Leticia accompanied her Agents to deal with the trash Sundae had removed from the Café.

Three weeks later, as the Country gathered around their television sets, their car radios, and near the White House lawn to hear the speech of the reigning President, the anticipation of the new and impending laws and regulations swirled with the hopes that many of the rumors would be true, and many more would be false.

Sundae Jones was sworn in as the new Vice President, as four Agents in Pink stood near the four Agents in Yellow at the side of the stage, with one Agent in White in the middle of the two groups. Leticia nodded to her Agents as they saluted back, then to Sundae who returned the nod with a hand over her heart, as the

President took the podium and microphone to address her Nation:

"My fellow Americans, I stand her today as not only your President, but as an American. I stand here today, as a Friend, Neighbor, Citizen, Sister, Daughter, and Leader, of a Nation that has once led by example, and has a chance once more, to lead, by example.." she said as she paused, looked at Sundae with a nod and wink, then at the building in the distance, and held up a hand.

The door to the building opened, with Holly exiting, and followed by a line of hooded figures, as they were led and marched towards the lawn and stage.

"We have done away with crime to a degree that we can once again, sleep with our doors unlocked. We have lowered our murder rate, by nearly ninety-percent!" Leticia demanded as she pounded the podium, "We have given incentives for jobs, and created safer streets!" she said as the line of hooded figures stopped before the stage, "And we have done all this, with adults in mind. Persons over the age of eighteen. But, what about those who feel the laws are beneath them, because the laws don't apply to them?" she asked, as she nodded to Holly, who began to walk the line, removing the hoods, and revealing the faces of youth.

"These, are not youth, they are adults, as of today" she said into the microphone, "Who have pretty much wasted the last several years of their lives, to be hooligans, thugs, assholes of society, because our laws don't apply to them.." she said with a snarl, "yet, this is where it begins.." she gestured to the individuals, "And today, is when it ends" she demanded as she pounded the podium, "Each of these, citizens.." she snarled as if the youth didn't deserve the title she had bestowed, "has watched since I took office, and knew our laws, our guidelines, our ways, and yet, none wanted to be a positive member of society, until they were forced to be.." she said as her gaze burned into their souls, "Forced, to be.." she snarled with intent at them, then stood tall, "So, as of today, ALL, Probation facilities for Youth and under-eighteen, will be closed, and all those collected will be sent to an 'off-site' location, and given a chance at repurposing their attention" she said as she cleared her throat, "the days of the parents being held responsible for their kids choices are done. The days of kids skipping school to vandalize, and the parents being held responsible, are over! The days of the youth terrorizing the streets for pleasure, are finished! Shape up, or be ready to be shipped out!" she screamed into the microphone, hearing the cheers above the jeers of those in attendance.

Leticia looked at Holly and nodded. Holly stepped in front of the first individual, and smiled as she followed the same example that Jake had all those years ago, as she asked the person their name, what they were in trouble for, and if they would commit that offense again. The first person shook so bad from being scared, they pissed and shit themselves, and fainted. The second, did the same from watching the first, and fell on top of the first in a pile. The third, was a big, brawny young man, who looked ten-years older than his birthday would suggest, standing with a chiseled grin, and an ego to match, as he refused to answer Holly's questions.

"You wont hurt me" the now-adult scoffed, "Your fat fingers wont even be able to pull the trigger, and don't get me started on that fat ass of yours" he laughed as he insulted Holly, "Let me outta these cuffs, and I will show you what a real man ca..".

BANG! Rang out the shot as Holly quickly pulled her Magnum, and fired a shot at the degrading-man's forehead.

The rest of the line popped to attention as the body fell.

"We are not joking, this is not a ruse" Leticia said as she watched Holly put her gun in its holster, and look at the next person in line, who was crying and kneeling, "If you want to play stupid games as kids and youth, you will win stupid prizes" she said as her smile grew, looking at the line of youth pop-to-attention, "disrespect the Authority and its laws, then this is where you will end up when you graduate from Nulla Reditus" she said as she pointed to the examples on the lawn, "This is a New America, a Proud America, a… Safe, America.." she said proudly as she pounded the podium, the cheers from the crowd filling the air, as Leticia looked as saw Holly walking back towards the building in the distance, her head hung-low, and her shoulders slumped.

The four Agents in Pink, and the four Agents in Yellow, left the stage and walked towards the line of youth, and stopped in a semi-circle near the lump of the two-fainted youth. One Agent in Yellow pointed to the first two youth in line, and then to the deceased lump of insults. The two youth jumped-to, grabbed the arms of the dead man, and began dragging it back towards the building slowly. The two Agents pointed to the next four youth in line, then to the two fainted youth, and waited as the four ran to the pile, unstacked them, and sat them up so they could be woke.

Leticia watched in silence for a few moments, nodded to the Agent in White, and the pair left the stage towards the White House, across the lawn, and through the doors of the Countries Capitol building.

Chapter 5

Sundae Jones was a middle-aged woman, with pale skin, blue eyes, and a killer-smile. While she had what most would consider a 'mom-bod', she held herself well, walked with pride, and loved who she was. She raised her kids alone, as the fathers of the children walked away early, yet she never seemed to struggle, and lived a life she and her kids could be proud of. Sundae had hopes and faith for society, and the youth of the next generations, but she knew there needed to be a shock to the system, and a wake-up call to the future of humanity.

The new Vice-President had asked to accompany Holly on her year-long task of closing the Youth Detention Facilities, and moving those 'Most Vulnerable to Regression' to the undisclosed location just off the Florida coast, known only as 'Nulla Reditus'.

Arriving in Flagstaff, Arizona, the last Friday of January just after the re-Inauguration, Holly, Sundae, and Moxie were escorted from the airport to the Youth Detention Facility, where they exited the large, dark-SUV wearing matching Black dresses, and matching Magnums on their hips. They were escorted to the door by two Agents in Pink, with Pink face-shields, and white head coverings. It was something Sundae was still getting used too.

"Do you ever get to see their faces?" Sundae asked as she walked behind Moxie and Holly, and patted the large handle on her hip, thinking it felt out of place somehow. Looking up, she couldn't help but notice Holly's large, swaying backside, and smiled at how it moved and danced under the dress.

Moxie shook her head, "Never, it's for their safety, and their families, ya' know?" she asked, glancing over her shoulder for a second towards the Vice-President, then forward again.

Sundae nodded as she thought about it, and turned her head to look at the Agents behind her, and smiled. The pair nodded in return, and walked in unison without skipping a beat. Sundae admired their stride for a moment, and looked forward again, noticing the intensity and seriousness of Holly as the thick woman in front of her walked, "Are you okay?" she asked, wanting to reach out to touch the 'Executioner', but hesitated.

Moxie looked at the VP quickly, and nodded, "She, is fine" she said quickly, but trying not to sound brash, "She has to, umm, disassociate herself from the feelings and emotions of her job and task, and today, is..

well, especially difficult and important.." she said as she slowed her pace a little to force Sundae to slow as well, then looking forward again, to see the line of Youth forming in the distance, along the wall towards the corner of the building.

Each Youth was lined up as the Convicts from the Prisons and Jails were when Leticia had started the release program in California eight years prior; Civilian clothes, backpack in one hand, Personnel and Medical File in the other.

"Why today?" Sundae asked quietly towards Moxie as their pace slowed, her hand now gripping the handle of the Magnum and definitely feeling as though it was not for her.

Moxie stopped, and held up her hand causing Sundae, and the Agents, to stop, allowing Holly to continue the walk alone up the long path to the Youth, "Those in Yellow shirts are over-eighteen, but have release issues, the rest in green shirts are under-eighteen, and its up to Holly to decide who gets the chance in Florida, and who gets to ride the Grey-Bus to nowhere.." she said quietly, "just so happens, she had her niece and nephew transferred here, so she could get them out of the way.." she said, looking at the VP with a sad expression, "She has hopes, but doubts how genuine the responses from the interview will be, and feels one will have to go, before the other realizes, its not a game" she whispered as she looked forward again, quieting as Holly began her interviews.

Sundae thought of what Moxie had just said, and released the handle of the large-gun on her hip. She looked at the line of Youth along the wall, the sprinkle of yellow shirts mixed in with the sea of green shirts, and wondered which had the strength to stay, and who would be at Holly's mercy. Then, looking at Holly, she wondered which of those before her were her niece and nephew, and her heart sank for the woman and the decision she would be forced to make.

Of the first twenty, only three were escorted to the Grey-Bus headed to Nulla Reditus, and only one Yellow-shirt met the end of Holly's final-decision maker. Of the next twenty, her niece and nephew were part of, and both were in Yellow. Holly took a deep breath, and had the next line step forward. Her niece, Kim, was third, and within minutes, two women stood just feet apart, yet were miles apart in every other aspect of life and views.

"Why, Kim?" Holly asked, exhaling as she shook her head, the idea of her task towards the emotionless teen making her almost sad.

The young and pretty blonde, who had an athletic figure and large breasts for a woman her age and size, stood there with an attitude of egotistical proportions that matched her bra-size, a smirk of disrespect forming on her face, "I heard your fat-ass had us transferred here" she said, spitting on the ground between them, and licking her lips, "just wasn't sure if your fat-ass would have the balls to show up here, and do this yourself, or if you would have the skinny-bitch over there handle us, because you're a pussy.." she said, spitting again as she sounded tough.

Holly took the abuse for a moment, shaking her head again, "You had every chance, every opportunity to do something with your life, and yet, here you are.." Holly said with sarcasm, "knocked up, what, eleven times, and had eleven abortions in three years?" she asked, chuckling a little as she shook her head in disbelief,

"Leading your brother on thefts, beatings, ditching school, and who the fuck knows what else, all while your parents take the blame and pay the fines?" she asked, bringing her hand up and placing it on the handle of her gun, tapping it with her index-finger.

Kim looked at the motion, and her demeanor changed instantly, as her eyes widened and began to turn red, "We didn't even have a chance! Mom lost her job, Dad began to drink.." she began, making excuses so she didn't have to accept the responsibility for her actions.

Holly smiled, "Which led you to steal, lie, cheat, and become less of a person? Rather than rise above it, and be better than them? Or, even better, helping the family out rather than being a burden on them, me, and society?" she asked, the tapping increasing as she looked down the line at her nephew, "and now, he gets to watch how fucking weak you really are, as you beg for your fucking life? Well done, Kim, well done.." she said, pulling her gun from her holster, and aiming it at her nieces forehead.

Kim dropped to her knees instantly, and began sobbing uncontrollably, the tears falling down her face as she cried out, "Please! Please! One more chance! Please! I will off myself if I fail!" she screamed as she pleaded with her Aunt, the tears falling to the ground.

Holly looked at the young woman on her knees, her hands clasped together, her head bowed, "You really think you can make amends for the last seven years of your bullshit?!" she questioned in a harsh tone, "all the shit you caused! All the hurt and pain!, and for what, Kim?! So you can be a bad ass to others who give two-fucks about you?!" she screamed as she paused, looking down the line to Tim, shaking her head, looking back at the knelt-Kim, lowering the barrel of her large Magnum pistol, and placing it to the back of her niece's head, "No, no, your time has come, and maybe, he will learn this lesson, and make things better.." she said, closing her eyes, and pulling the trigger.

The bullet went through the back of Kim's head, exiting her face, the flesh and blood coating the ground as the bullet lodged in Kim's leg. The body of the victim fell to the side, as the gasps of shock flooded the line. Holly opened her eyes, wiped the heavy-stream of tears with her sleeve, looked down the line, and saw each Youth was standing at attention, and a frightened look on their faces. She knew it would only take one sacrifice, and was devastated it was her niece.

Holly holstered her piece, took a step back, turned, and walked between the VP and Moxie, "I think we are done here.." she said mournfully as she walked towards the vehicles, her head slightly down.

Moxie and Sundae looked at each other as Holly walked between them, then at the Youth as they lined the wall and walkway, as the Vice President gave a wave to the Officers who led them, and a slight-nod too release the youth, and let them rejoin their families who were waiting outside the tall, chain-linked fence. The two women turned and followed Holly to the vehicles, loaded up, and drove back to the airport in silence.

Boarding the plane, and finding her seat, Holly spun her chair around so she faced away. Moxie and Sundae found seats towards the back, buckled their seatbelts, and waited silently for the Attendant to check on them. The plane's engines started with a gentle-rumble, and began whirling faster and louder, as the lights in the cabin blinked off, then back on, and the small crew and passengers were ready to take off. Within fifteen minutes, the plane was at its forty-thousand-foot cruising altitude, and headed towards D.C.

Holly spun around in her chair slowly, and looked at the two ladies near the rear of the plane, shook her head in shame and embarrassment, unbuckled her seatbelt, stood, and began walking slowly towards her friends.

"You think she's okay?" Sundae whispered to Moxie as she watched the thick-hipped woman sway towards them.

Moxie smiled and nodded gently, "That's the toughest bitch I have ever met" she whispered back, "Give her time.." she said and paused, as Holly stopped in the isle a row before the ladies seats.

Holly tapped the earpiece in her ear, and slightly shook her head, "Sorry, Mox.." she said, the look on her face as serious as she had ever been, "You gotta die.." she said as she shook her head, and tapped the handle of her gun.

Sundae and Moxie looked at each other in shock, as the planes engines spun loudly outside the plane. Two Agents in Pink stood, and walked towards the rear and ladies, prompting Moxie to stand. She was placed under arrest, with her hands behind her back, a black hood over her head, and lead to the front of the plane, to a seat with extra shackles.

"What the fuck, Holly? Really?" Sundae asked, standing to object.

"This comes from the President, Madam Vice President" Holly said, holding a hand up to stop her, "but, there is a situation in Israel with the Hamas, that needs our attention.." she said to change the subject.

Sundae watched as Moxie was shackled to her chair, the dark hood covering he face and blonde hair, as several beeps could be heard through the cabin of the plane, "And give her a piece of chocolate from her pocket, will ya?" she asked compassionately, "We don't need her going into DKA and dying before we can get this... figured out" she said as she waved her hands in the air in circles, then turning her attention to Holly quickly, "Israel?" she asked, "Who started it?" she asked, looking nervous.

Holly's face looked worried for a moment, "Think, 9/11.." she said, looking over her shoulder at the seated and hooded Moxie, at the Agents in Pink, then back to Sundae, "It gets a little more complicated than that" she said, and offered Sundae to take her seat, as she sat on the other side of the isle, leaned over with her arm resting on the armrest, and talked as the engines whirled outside the plane.

The next day, Leticia took the stage and podium in front of the White House, the cameras from the News Agencies all in attendance, as the President began on that chilly, sunny Tuesday, "My fellow patriotic Americans.." she began as she looked down at her notes, then back to the cameras, "we are saddened by the events in Israel and Gaza, the people and horrific crimes against humanity that are being dealt to civilians by a evil and corrupt system.." she said, as the door to the far building opened, Holly exited wearing a Yellow dress and black boots, her gun on her side, followed by a figure in a hood, escorted by four Agents in Yellow, and one Agent in White, "and as we know, corruption comes in many, many forms.." she said as Holly stopped on the lawn in her traditional spot, the hooded-figure positioned against the wall, and the Agents in a semi-circle behind Holly, "and while one of our own helped in the orchestration of said events, that too, needs to be dealt with swiftly, as our hands are tied with interfering in the events in Israel, they are free to deal the harsh and swift realities of justice here" she said as she nodded to Holly.

Holly removed her gun from her holster, aimed it at the hooded-figure, and pulled the trigger. The round hit its mark, as the hooded-figure fell back with a thud, blood soaking and filling the hood, before oozing through the fabric, and joining the other stains from the executions before. Holly holstered her weapon, nodded to Leticia, and walked back to the building followed by the five Agents.

"And now, we will turn our attention to the victims, and civilians in Gaza.." Leticia said as she turned her gaze from the bloodied flesh, and looked deep into the cameras once more, "and so help me, we will hold everyone accountable, regardless of Government, and their so-called Leaders.." she said sternly into the cameras, her face stern as her eyes squinted, and her brow furrowed, "Ready or not, here we come.." she said as she pounded the podium, and exited the small stage, down the steps, towards the White House, and the waiting Agent in White.

Chapter 6

The first five-years of Leticia Gonzalez's Presidential terms had changed the country, shocked the People, and altered the future of a Nation that had once been deemed 'A burden of hatred'. With the executions on the White House Lawn becoming less and less frequent, the fact that they were still happening showed the world the United States had a vision for a better future, and the World needed to be alert and ready for the change that was about to come.

It had been nearly two months since the latest execution on the front lawn, and while the desk of Moxie sat empty for those two months, her presence was still deep in the halls of the Government's Home. The events in the Middle-East had worsened, and while the Governments of the World pointed fingers and placed blame on who started the war and attacks, Leticia was ready to tell NATO to go to hell, and she would step in.

The first Monday of May 2037, Leticia entered her Oval Office, with the Joint Chiefs waiting for her on the sofas and chairs in her office. As she entered, and paused, she was taken back by a familiar face near her desk, holding a cup of coffee, and a file. Letty smiled as she approached her desk, and took her cup of hot liquid.

"Good morning" the President said cheerfully to the woman behind her chair.

"Good morning, Madam President" the new assistant replied as she handed the white mug and file over to her Boss.

Letty looked at the name-badge that hung around the new woman's neck, took notice of the name, and smiled, "Roxie?" she asked, pulling the cup to her lips, and taking a sip, "Ya know, you remind me of someone.." she said, setting the cup on her desk, pulling the chair out, and plopping the file on the desk next to the cup.

Roxie had a slim build, small breasts, blonde hair, and a smile that could stop a truck. Her brown eyes sparkled as she smiled, and while she wasn't exactly tall, her heels added the inches she needed to feel as though she belonged. She was the spitting image of Moxie, and while she was new and nervous, she knew she would fit in if given a chance.

Leticia sat as she smiled at Roxie, and watched the new assistant walk towards the door, exit, and close the door behind her.

"You think it was a good idea to hire the traitors twin?" a General asked as he shifted on the sofa.

Leticia's smile faded at the question, as she reached for her cup, and raised it to her mouth, her eyes glaring over the rim at the General intently, taking a sip, and setting the cup down, "Do you know what she did?" she asked, interlocking her fingers on her desk.

The Joint Chiefs looked at each other in silence.

"No, I didn't think so, so shut the fuck up of things out of your paygrade, huh?" Leticia demanded as she unlocked her fingers, and picked up the folder in front of her, opening it, and glancing at the pages, "So, Israel faked the attacks?" she asked, looking up at the General again, "Is that real, or are you speculating?" she asked, glancing at the pages again, setting the first one on the desk, and reading the next page.

"Yes, Ma'am" an Admiral replied from a chair, "We captured a woman, who claims to be the daughter of one of the Palestine leaders, and she said her brother, and another man who was the son of the Israeli Prime Minister, set up the attacks with the help of Iran.." he said, looking at the other Joint Chiefs for approval.

Leticia read for a moment, and looked up at the nodding heads, "Iran..?" the President asked, looking at the page again, then back to the Admiral, "Where is this woman?" she asked, reaching for her cup.

The Joint Chiefs looked at each other, as the Admiral spoke, "She, is currently on the Island with the Youth of America" he said with a hint of worry.

Leticia set her cup down, and the file, a look of disgust coming over her face, "What the actual fuck is wrong with you people?!" she demanded, standing quickly as the chair shot out behind her, hitting the small table behind the desk and making the Presidential-Bust of JFK shake on the small table, "You treat her like a criminal?" she screamed as she punched the desk, making her knuckles pop.

The Joint Chiefs each looked at each other, sweat building on each of their brows as they looked for the words that would keep them from the lawn, wall, and Holly.

Leticia stood there, snarling at the uniformed men around her, "You have one-hour to have her in that chair" she said, pointing to the chair the Admiral was in, "or each of you takes her place in her hell of a cell" she said, reaching for her seat, and pulling it to her backside as she sat, glaring at those around her, "what are you waiting for?!" she screamed as she watched the uniformed men jump from their seats, and rush to the door to leave.

Leticia watched them scurry away like rats after the last piece of cheese, as she leaned back in her chair, spun to face the windows, and rub her temples of the pain that was forming in her head. With the door open, and Roxie standing at the doorway waiting patiently, Leticia closed her eyes and answered, "What can I do for you?" she asked blindly.

Roxie took a few slow and shorts steps into the Office, "There is a, Uncle Larry, on the phone for you, Madam President.." she said with a hint of confusion in her voice.

Leticia opened her eyes for a moment, the sunny day blinding her through the windows as she spun in her chair, looked at Roxie in her green dress and heels, smiled, and looked at the flashing light on the Presidential phone, "Thank you, Roxie, that will be all" she replied as the light flashed.

Roxie smiled and nodded, taking a few steps backwards, and closing the door.

Leticia took a deep breath, reached for the phone, and picked up the receiver as she placed it to her ear, "Larry.." she said casually as she reached for her cup.

There was a silence on the other end for a moment, then some heavy breathing for a moment, "You really have no clue what the fuck you are doing, do you?" the male voice of Larry sounded in a harsh tone.

Leticia chuckled as she took a sip, and set her cup down, "And what makes you say that, Larry?" she asked, leaning back and gently rocking in her large, leather chair, a slight chuckle bellowing from her, "You were the one who tanked Wall Street, because you wanted to throw a temper-tantrum over the closure of the prisons.." she laughed, and paused as she moved the receiver to her other ear.

Larry scoffed on the other end of the phone, his breathing getting heavier, "You killed my son" he grunted into the phone.

Leticia laughed as she threw her head back, nearly dropping the receiver, "You want to go back and forth, tit-for-tat, with me about why we did the things we did? You senile fuck.." she said as her tone became serious quick, "I brought Wall Street back to the People, I repurposed those businesses and buildings you closed and bankrupt" she snarled as her eyes narrowed, "I gave the fucking People what they wanted, needed, deserved.." she demanded into the phone, taking a deep breath as she began to compose herself, brushing her blouse of wrinkles, and leaning forward slightly in her chair towards ther desk.

Larry listened intently for a moment, and snickered, "I'm glad you think your winning" he said with a chuckle, "Keep that egotistical-momentum, Letty.." he said in an almost whisper, "Because Moxie won't be the only innocent sacrifice you will make because of bad intel.." he said with another chuckle, and hung up the phone.

Leticia listened to the phone hang up on the other end, looked at the receiver, and laughed as she hung up the phone. Reaching for her cup, she heard a knock at her door, "Yeah?" she said loudly as she took a sip from her cup, and set it down.

The door opened, and there stood Roxie, with a wide smile on her face, "Ma'am, The Agent is here to see you.." she said sweetly, stepping back and allowing the Agent in White to emerge.

The Agent wore a White suit, Fedora, with a whilte face-shield and head-wrap, but the tie and gloves were Purple, and the boots were black. The Agent carried a folder and a file in one hand, and a small box in the other.

Leticia smiled, and waved the Agent in, "Thank you, Roxie" she said as the Agent entered, and sat in the chair opposite the President's desk, "What can I do for you?" she asked.

The Agent leaned forward, setting the folder and file on the desk, and placing the small box on top, gently sliding it towards the President, without a word.

Leticia smiled for a moment, "You know, White looks better on you" she said with a chuckle, reaching for the file and pulling the small stack towards her, "Things going okay down there?" she asked, sliding the small box from the short stack of manila, and opening the file.

The Agent nodded, and sat tall in the comfy chair, running the gloved hands along the soft leathered-armrests a few times.

"I know, I love that chair" Leticia said with a chuckle, turning her attention to the papers in front of her, "Wow, that, that is impressive" she said as she shook her head, and looked up at the Agent, "And, these are current?" she asked and paused.

The Agent nodded, and gave a thumbs-up, setting the hand back on the arm, and stroking it a little.

"You miss it here?" the President asked, sensing something from the person across from her.

The Agent raised their right hand flat, and gave it a little shake.

"Yeah.." Leticia said with a smile and head-nod, "We miss you here too" she said reassuringly, "But, it was, and is, important that you gave that sacrifice, ya' know?" she asked, hoping the Agent understood.

The Agent stood quickly, nodded, and placed their right hand over their heart, as they stood at attention, before sitting once more.

Leticia smiled and chuckled to herself, "I don't know how I got so lucky, but I sure am glad I was in that bar that night" she said, turning her attention back to the papers, "Implement another program or two for rewarding good-behavior and incentives, and maybe, we can save more of them than we thought or hoped.." she said, closing the file and sliding it to the side, then looking at the Agent.

The Agent nodded in agreement.

Leticia smiled, "Good, now.." she said as she reached for her letter opener for the envelope, "Am I going to like this?" she asked, forcing the opener in the crease of the fold, and ripping into it.

The Agent shook their head from side-to-side.

Leticia paused as the opener finished through the large envelope, set the sharp instrument down, and paused, "Is it as bad as I think?" she asked.

The Agent didn't move.

"Are you fucking kidding me?" she asked, opening the envelope, and withdrawing the few papers, and beginning to read them, "yadda yadda yadda.." she repeated as she scanned the first page, and stopped about halfway, "They are bringing me the woman in a bit, I want you here for that, you understand me?" she asked, sounding stern.

The Agent nodded and stood.

"Hold on" Leticia said as she turned her attention back to the page in her hand, and read quickly, setting the first page down, and beginning the second. As she reached the bottom of the page, her jaw began to lower, and her mouth gapped open in shock at the news in her hands, "Get the fuck outta here" she said as she set the second page down, and began the third page, pausing, and setting it down, "Be back here in an hour, and have the teams ready to go by Thursday" she said, looking up at the Agent as she rubbed her temple from frustration at what she just read.

The Agent in White nodded, saluted, and turned to leave.

"Don't let anything happen to her, please" Leticia said quickly.

The Agent paused, nodded, and continued to the door, reaching the handle, pulling the door open, and exiting past the Assistant's desk and out of view.

"Roxie?" Leticia announced towards the open door.

A moment later, the pretty-blonde emerged with a smile, "Yes Ma'am?" she asked, standing alert with a pen and pad of paper in her hands.

Leticia laughed as she saw a familiarity before her, "We are going to have some guests in a bit, please make sure we have some tea and a small dish of Middle Eastern cuisine, please?" she asked, and watched as Roxie scribbled.

"Yes Ma'am" the blonde replied as she wrote quickly, "Anything else?" she asked, finishing up and looking up at her Boss behind the chair.

Leticia thought for a moment, and smiled, "No, thank you, that will be all" she said with a nod, and watched as Roxie smiled, nodded in return, and left the room leaving the door open.

Leticia looked at the clock, saw she had time, and left to the kitchen for food, and a break, knowing she was going to be knee-deep in a situation with no end in sight for some time to come.

An hour later, returning to her office, and sitting at her desk, Leticia was alerted by Roxie that the Joint Chiefs, and their guest, were on their way. Leticia thanked Roxie, stood and walked to the side-bar, and poured a small shot of whiskey, drank it, exhaled loudly and laughed, then walked to her desk and leaned against it to wait.

A few minutes later, two Generals entered the office, followed by the Agent in White with a Purple tie, a woman with Olive-skin and jet-black hair, an Agent in Yellow, and the remaining Joint Chiefs. The small group entered the Oval Office, sat in chairs, and let the Guest have the middle of the room, and the comfy-leather chair.

Leticia looked at her team of uniformed men, the two Agents behind her, and then at her Guest, "You know who I am?" she asked, placing her hand gently on her chest.

The woman nodded with a smirk, "The world knows who you are" she said sweetly in a thick-accent, a smile on her face as well, "and thank you, for letting me speak" she said, bowing her head slowly, and raising it again out of respect.

Leticia looked at her team of advisors, and shook her head, then looked at the woman, "And you are, Sham'az Hala Farhat? Did I pronounce that correctly?" she asked, hoping she didn't butcher it too badly and insult the guest.

The woman smiled and nodded, "Sha'maz Allah Farhat, but close enough for bad intel" she laughed as she too looked at the men around her.

Leticia smiled, rose from her spot, and walked to her seat behind her desk to sit, "And you know, what happened?" she asked, sitting.

Sha'maz nodded as she licked her lips, "It was treason from the beginning" she said, licking her lips again.

Leticia noticed the action, and held up her finger, "Can we get her some water, or tea, and those snacks?

Roxie?" she said loudly, and smiled when the blonde emerged from the door.

"Ma'am? The snacks?" Roxie asked sweetly with a smile, nodded, and left to retrieve the requested items.

Leticia nodded and winked as she gave a 'finger-gun-shoot' to her new assistant, "You are amazing, Rox" she said, watching Roxie leave, and looking back at her guest, "Please, continue.." she offered with a soft-smile.

Sha'maz smiled and nodded slightly, "My brother was in the office when he overheard the Isaerli Prime Minister on the phone with the Palestinian Prime Minister, the Iranian President, the Leader of Hamas, and a man with an American accent.." she said, closing her eyes to remember, "Larry.." she said as if it was moments ago, the memory fresh in her head.

Leticia looked next to her at the Agent in White with a stern look, then back to her guest, "What did your brother hear?" she asked, looking at the Joint Chiefs and seeing they were all ears and alert.

The Guest shook her head as she lowered it, memories flooding her head as the tears began to fall down her face to her pants, "Israel would attack themselves, and blame Hamas, forcing the people to retreat into the most crowded areas, and both sides would then begin the assault, claiming each had started it, and that the enemy was in Gaza.." she said through tears, her head still down as her sobs filled the room.

The Joint Chiefs squirmed in their seats as they listened to the guest describe the atrocities that were being committed, with their intel correct from the beginning about who started the attacks, the Joint Chiefs looked at each other, and shifted nervously in their chairs, as to who to blame for something each of them could have stopped or at least prolonged, before thousands of innocent people were slaughtered. The Attacks on Pearl Harbor, and the warnings they had then, made this scenario feel as though it could have been thwarted, and wasn't.

Leticia shook her head, looked at the door as Roxie, the Assistant, entered with the tray of tea packets, hot water, and snacks that would be considered 'comfort food' of the Middle East. The President nodded to the Admiral to help the guest leave the room, and follow

Roxie to the side office. The room was quiet for a few moments as the guest followed behind Roxie to leave the Office, as the Admiral returned to his seat, and the room was secured for a private meeting.

Leticia stood, and smacked her desk, "You, mother fuckers, are all fired!" she screamed as she looked around to each of them, "and I don't mean, lose your job from here fired.." she snarled as she leaned across her desk, "Each of you will be striped to E-1 of your respective branches, given 30 days in the brig, bread and water for three of them every ten days, and given the shittiest jobs for the next five years, without pay, without advancement.." she snarled as she wanted to think of more, and couldn't, "Get them the fuck outta here" she grunted as she flung her hand in the air, pointing to the door, "and be fucking grateful you fuckers aren't executed on that fucking lawn out there!" she demanded as she pointed out the window towards the stage and stained lawn.

Several Agents in Yellow, and an Agent in Pink entered the room swiftly, and began to gather the now excused Joint Chiefs from their seats, and escort them from the Office, when the Agents in White and Pink was halted.

"Hand them off to the Agents at the end of the hall, and you two return, please?" Leticia asked through a frustrated and burdened tone, her anger and frustration exhuming from her as she waited.

The Agents nodded, left the room briefly, and returned.

Leticia walked around her desk to her chair, and stood behind it as she looked at the two masked individuals before her, "Four teams, four targets, one night.." she said as she looked at them, holding up four-fingers for clarification, "Seals, Recon, Rangers, You, got it?" she asked with clarity so there was no room for misinterpretation.

The Agents nodded in agreement.

"Good" Leticia said as she pulled her chair, and sat, "I only want those evil fuckers who are behind this, the rest, well.." she said as she reached for her pen and a piece of paper, "the ones who are against the leaders, will probably be in jails or torture-compounds, right?" she asked, making a quick note of names of the Leaders and Heads of Monarchies to collect or kill, folding the paper in half, and handing it to the Agent in White.

The Agents nodded as they understood, as the Agent in White took the paper, and slid it in a jacket pocket.

Leticia opened her desk drawer, and withdrew a small, round, clear-plastic case, and shook it gently, making it rattle, "1871" she said as she tossed the coin on the desk, "Bring me Larry while your at it" she said, moving her attention from the coin to her Agents, watching them nod in unison, and leave her Office. She turned her attention back to the coin, reached out and flicked it with her right index finger and watched it slide away from her on her desk, and remembered she had a guest.

Rising from her seat, Leticia walked to the side door, opened it, and saw a happy and content Sha'maz sipping tea, and reading a newspaper.

"Comfortable?" Leticia asked, a smile on her face seeing her troubled guest at ease.

Sha'maz looked up from her paper and smiled, "Much better, thank you" she said in a thick Middle Eastern accent, "but your tea.." she said, contorting her face queerly.

Leticia chuckled and nodded, "Note taken" she replied as she entered the room, and walked to the seat across from her guest, "Can we talk?" she asked, smoothing her suit as she sat.

Sha'maz set her cup and newspaper down, and sat a little taller, "Of course" she replied, her accent thick as she too smoothed her attire.

Leticia smiled at the attempt, "We have been watching the routines of those in charge over there, and I gotta know.." she said as serious as she could, "What are we walking into, that we cant see?" she asked, knowing the information could change everything.

The guest knew the question was coming, as she smiled, and reached into her back pocket, removing a small, folded piece of paper, "There is a birthday in July" she said as she handed the paper over, "All of them will be there.." she said as she watched Leticia take the paper.

The President held the folded-paper in her right hand, looking at it with a confused face, "Who is 'all of them'?" she asked as she began to unfold the paper, and saw a list that filled the page.

"The ones you want, the leaders.." she said, her tone serious as she watched Leticia read the names, and title in the government.

Leticia read slowly, realizing she had just written down many of the names and handed them to the Agent in White, but also seeing new names on the checklist of corrupt-terror she held, "That's less than eight-weeks away.." she stated as she began to smile, folding the paper, and sliding it in her pocket, looking at Sha'maz as sincere as she could, "How much danger would you be in if you went back?" she asked, her face showing as much compassion as it could.

Sha'maz closed her eyes, and shook her head, "My brother was killed because of what he knew, and my family was killed for what they might know.." she said with her eyes closed, before opening them as a few tears began to fall for the loved ones she lost, "no one is safe, no one will survive if those men stay in power.." she said, looking away as she closed her eyes again, wiping her face.

Leticia watched her guest become emotional and vulnerable, as she reached for the box of tissue next to her, and placed it on the cushion next to Sha'maz, "Listen, we have a safe-place for you to go for a while, okay? Just be patient, and relax, you're safe now.." she reassured with a soft smile.

Sha'maz wiped her face with her hands again, and looked at Leticia, "Safe?" she asked, looking down at the box of tissues, grabbing one, wiping her eyes again, and blowing her nose lightly, wiping it, and looking at the President, "None of us are safe as long as that Larry-guy, is in charge over there" she said, her face red, but her voice stern.

"Who's birthday is it?" Leticia asked, reaching over and pulling another tissue, and handing it to her guest.

Sha'maz took the tissue carefully, and smirked gently, "Larry's, of course" she said in her accent as she wiped her face one last time, and sat straight up, "I want to go.." she said firmly, dropping the tissue to the floor between her feet.

Leticia was taken-back as she sat taller for a moment, the look of shock on her face, "Back?" she asked, her brow furrowing with questions, "For what?" she asked, looking around the room to see if they were still alone, and they were.

Sha'maz chuckled and shook her head, pausing briefly to let the question swirl in the air between them, "I have, ummm, a present for him" she said as she nodded slowly, the smirk growing into a devious smile.

Leticia looked up at her guest, and noticed the woman was rubbing her belly, and there was the slightest of bumps, "You're, pregnant?" she asked, placing her hand over her mouth,

Sha'maz looked down at her host, the twinkle in her eye said more than any word could, as she bent down for her small bag, stood slowly, and walked towards the door to leave, stopping, and turning to look at Leticia, "Please, get us there safe, and I promise, I will get you in safe when the time comes" she offered, smiling with a nod as she rubbed her belly again, and left through the Oval Office, towards the desk of Roxie.

Leticia let the news sink in, as she lowered her hand from her mouth, and shook her head. She thought of her Joint Chiefs and their lack of intel for not only the situation in Gaza, but the pregnancy of the woman. She stood from her seat, shook her head again to regain her composure, and walked back into her office, where she was met by the Agent in White, and the Agent in Yellow from earlier, "Did, did you two hear that shit?" she asked, scoffing at the news as she walked to the side-bar to pour a drink, "You, think she's lying?" she asked reaching the bar, and pulling the crystal top off a decanter, "You think she's playing us?" she asked, lifting the decanter to pour her short drink.

The two Agents looked at each other for a moment, paused, and turned their attention back to their Boss, and shrugged.

Leticia picked up her glass of Whiskey, swirled it gently to release the aroma, and chuckled at the 'shoulder-shrug', "Listen.." she said in a happily-sarcastic tone as she turned and looked at the Agents, "I expect that shit from them fuckers" she said, thumbing towards the door, and taking a sip, exhaling the sharp-bite of the Whiskey, and walking slowly to her seat, "But, you..?" she asked, looking at the Agent in White as she set her glass down and sat, pulling the chair towards her rear, "Please, tell me.." she said in a soft and vulnerable tone.

The Agent in White looked at the Agent in Yellow, gave a head tilt, stepped forward a step, and nodded their head, 'Yes'.

"We are not waiting for July" Leticia said as she reached for her drink, as she thought about the head-nod, took a sip, and looked at the Agent in Yellow, "Fuck, I wish you Agents could talk" she laughed, "You can go, thank you" she said to the Agent in Yellow, "And close the door behind you, please" she said as she looked at and pointed to the Agent in White, "You, stay, and sit" she said, watching the other Agent leave towards the door, as Leticia got up from her seat, and followed, looking at the Agent in White as the Agent sat in the comfy, leather chair opposite the large desk, "We, have some things to talk about" she said, reaching the door, locking it, and turning to the Agent in the room, "and trust me, we are going to talk" she said with a chuckle, walking back to her desk.

On Thursday, several days later, Leticia met in her Office with the newly-appointed Joint Chiefs, and was pleased to see half of them were female. Not that she was opposed to men, but with the last several years of her Political career as an example, she knew it was good to have persons of compassion. The General of the Army, and the Admiral of the Navy were both women, and had risen through the ranks of their branches with distinction, as well as having reputations for being 'Mavericks', or 'Renegades', and going against orders to make sure the mission succeeded, and more lives didn't end needlessly.

Next to Leticia stood the Agent in Pink, with the tie sharp and shiny Green, and next to the Agent was the Agent in Yellow, with the tie Green and Sharp. Both of the Agents gloves matched the tie, as the boots were both steel-toed and Government issue for the Special Forces.

"Our Guest is on her way back to Israel.." Leticia announced in almost frustration, as she leaned across her desk, exhaling deeply as the sun shone through the windows of the office, "and from what we hear, she is pregnant with Uncle Larry's baby.." she scoffed as if the news was unbelievable, rolling her eyes as she chuckled, "but our intel tells us she has a tumor, and is dying.." she said, sitting taller and sounding more positive.

The Joint Chiefs looked at each other for a moment, then at the President, then looked down at their leather-bound notebooks as they flipped them open to read what they were hearing.

"You won't find what I'm telling you in those old reports" Leticia said clearly as she motioned for the new information to be distributed amongst the new Joint Chiefs.

The Agent in Pink left from behind the desk, and emerged holding a stack of files, handing one to each of the Uniformed Officers, then returned to the spot behind the desk.

Leticia shook her head and smirked, as she looked behind her at the Agent in Yellow, scribbled a note on a paper, folded it, and handed it to the Agent, "Make sure this is taken care of, quickly, please" she asked, and watched as the Agent in Yellow took the note, nodded, and left towards the door of the Oval Office.

The Joint Chiefs watched the Agent leave, and turned their attentions back to the files in their laps, as they opened them, and began reading in horror.

"That's right" Leticia announced as she watched the faces of the Uniformed Staff turn to sadness, disbelief, and frustration, "Israel and Palestine, with Hamas, agreed to a three-day cease-fire so they could get as many civilians and Americans out of Gaza.." she said as she stood, and turned to look out the Office windows to the lawn and permanent podium and stage, "and at the end of the first day, with over two-hundred thousand fleeing, the three opened fire.." she said mournfully as the news was almost to tragic to share, "killing nearly all of them, and blaming each other for the attack.." she finished as she turned around, the sun behind her as she stood tall.

The Uniformed Staff listened as they read the reports, finished and looked at each other, then at the President as she was handed a tissue from the Agent in Pink, "What do you recommend, Madam President?" the

Admiral asked as she closed her folder, and placed her hands in her lap on the folder.

There was a knock, and the sound of a throat clearing from the door, as the Staff and President looked, and saw Holly standing and waiting patiently, and smiling, wearing a blue dress that hugged her wide hips, and engulfed the large mounds on her chest. Her hair was pulled back and held by a wrap that covered her ears, her make-up light, as she took a step into the Office, "Madam President, Joint Chiefs.." she said as she entered, and stopped, nodding to the group, "The Strike-Teams are assembled, and ready to go, Ma'am.." she said, lowering her arms to her side, and waiting.

The Joint Chiefs looked at each other in confusion as their brows furrowed, and they looked at the President with awkward scowls.

Leticia turned and nodded to Holly, as she looked at her Staff of Uniformed Officers as they sat confused, "The less you know, the better.." she said as she paused, "We are not going to go to war over this, we are not going to sacrifice thousands of lives and billions of dollars over this" she said as she sat at her desk, and looked at Holly,

"Is the War-Room ready?" she asked as she reached for a pen from the container on the desk.

Holly nodded sharply, "Ma'am, and the Agents are on stand-by ready for your command" she said as she stood tall.

Leticia nodded as she made a note, folded the paper, and slid it into the top drawer as she looked up at the clock on the wall, "Fifteen minutes" she said as she looked at Holly for clarification.

"Fifteen minutes, yes Ma'am" Holly replied with a nod, glanced at the Staff, smiled, and turned to leave, stopping at the desk of Roxie for a quiet and quick chat before leaving to her task.

Leticia stood from her desk, looked at the Admiral, and then the clock again, "Fifteen minutes, be at the War-Room" she said sharply, before walking towards the door to leave, "Dismissed.." she said over her shoulder as she left through the door, followed by the Agent in White.

The dark room held FOUR large television screens that were attached to head-mounts of soldiers, a half-dozen smaller ones that were connected to satellites, and many more computer monitors that had many other screens of soldiers, compounds, vehicles, and more, that were being monitored by Agents in Pink, as the President and Admiral, along with Holly and Roxie, stood by and watched.

Three of the four screens had Yellow Agents as the Person in charge of the Operation, while the fourth was a Agent in White with a Purple tie, followed by an Agent in Yellow in a Pink tie. As soon as Leticia gave the command, the teams on screen embarked on their missions, with minimal gunfire or action for the first few minutes. Then, without warning, war on all four screens erupted for several minutes, and as fast as it began, it stopped.

"Bunker secure" the Operation-Leaders sounded off one-by-one, as the smoke cleared and the scenes and screens came clear and into focus. Each room had several deceased guards in Middle-Eastern uniforms, as well as persons of interest in suits draped over chairs and tables, with several in cuffs and laying on the floor, "Package in hand, headed to the LZ" each Team Leader said as they left their respective rooms, with moments later an explosion behind them destroying the scene.

The screens showed the Teams running to their escape vehicles, driving swiftly through the streets of their respective areas of the Middle East, stopping in fields and running towards large Helicopters, shutting doors, and lifting off as the four Leaders gave 'thumbs-up's', and the screens went blank.

The Admiral stood shocked for a moment, and looked at Leticia, "What, the fuck, just happened?" she asked as she looked at the blank screens, "You know what you just did?" she asked, looking back at her Boss with a look of horror and disbelief on her face.

Leticia smiled and nodded a smug smile, "Just wait, and I will tell you what 'We' just did" she replied as she looked at the watch on her wrist, then at the door.

The door opened, and entered Sundae, the Vice President, "Have they checked in yet?" she asked as she walked down the short set up steps and joined the four women.

"Not yet, Ma'am" Roxie replied anxiously as she rocked on her heels.

Holly interrupted, "Should be any minute, Ma'am" she said walking towards one of the Agents at the stations, and whispering in their ear.

Seconds later, all four of the large screens turned on, and there stood the Agent in White, with the Agent in Yellow next to them, both at attention, and their attire dirty from the operation.

"How did it go?" Leticia asked.

The Agent in White shrugged, removing the face-shield and fedora, and pulling the head-covering back, revealing the Bartender from Gasquet, "Larry wasn't here Ma'am, and that Sha'maz lady is dead" he reported sternly, still trying to catch his breath as he wiped his forehead of the sweat from the mission.

Leticia shook her head, "And the others?" she asked, sounding frustrated and perturbed.

The Agent in White stroked his red beard that was in two braids that hung from his chin, "They are on their way to Nulla Reditus" he said as he nodded.

Two-sets of beeps sounded next to the Agent in White, coming from the Agent in Yellow, as the Agent pulled their phone, looked at it, and put the phone back in the pocket it was retrieved from.

"I swear, Moxie, that CGM is going to get you killed" Leticia laughed as she watched the Agent in Yellow remove their fedora, visor, and pull back the head-covering as well, reveling the slender face and blonde hair of the former-Secretary, Moxie.

Moxie chuckled with a slight head-bow, "Yes, Ma'am.." she replied as she placed her Fedora under her left arm, "Rox" she said to her near-twin.

"Cousin" Roxie replied with a smile and nod, "I'm not sure I want to give you this job back" she laughed as she looked at Holly, who smirked and nodded.

"Come back soon" Holly nodded and smirked with a wink.

Moxie laughed and nodded, "Give us a few weeks, there's still some shit to do here" she said business-like, and looked at the man next to her.

The Agent in White nodded, "The head is gone, Ma'am, but we got who and what we came for.." he said as he placed the Fedora on his head, adjusted it, and shook his head slightly, "There was a file, Ma'am.." he said, scoffing at the news he was about to share.

Leticia looked confused for a moment, "Just one?" she chuckled, and stopped when she saw the Agent wasn't smiling, "Should I be worried, or mad?" she asked, shifting her weight.

The Agent in White glared at the camera as he held up the file, "The Speaker of the House, is working on a coup.." he said as he shook the file in his hand, "Larry has taken the steps to remove you, and it seems, by force.." he said as he lowered the file from the camera, and waited.

Leticia looked at the Admiral, Sundae Jones, Roxie and Holly, then back at the screen with her Agents looking back at her, "Drop them off at Nulla, and get back here.." she said sternly, "bring me the file, and the Speaker.." she said as she watched the Agents nod, and the screen go black with a multi-colored line through the middle.

Chapter 7

Hating the world, or society and its people, often has a beginning that has been learned, usually from someone that is viewed as a mentor, public figure, or relative. When that hatred, or negative view, is accepted and adopted as one's daily practice, a potential future of faith is immediately altered, a family dynamic is changed, and what should have been, is changed to a 'what could have been'. For Larry, this was no different.

Larry was the middle grandchild to one of the most ruthless men, his Grandfather Bernard Fisqual, who had inherited the 'Family Business' when he too was a young man, and was molded by his Father, and Grandfather, as well. All had been taught the tough lessons of life, hardened by the choices from those before them, and shown there was no room for compassion for society, or life other than those with the Fisqual name.

When Larry was seven, he accompanied his father, Lawrence Sr., to the large, magnificent home of his Grandfather Bernard. The weather that day was one of the worst storms the East Coast of America had endured in the early Twentieth Century, with rain falling by the sheets, and the visibility on the road near zero.

Arriving at the large mansion that rivaled the White House in Washington D.C., Larry always exited the vehicle, and looked up in awe. While his home with his parents was magnificent, visiting his Grandfather's home was always like going to a New York Hotel. Larry and his father exited the vehicle under a large umbrella, and strolled across the large driveway, up the long-flight of stairs towards the elaborate front doors, and were greeted by the traditional Butler who's family had been serving the Fisqual's for what seemed the beginning of time.

As the door to the large home opened, a handsomely-older Black man stood, with his hair turning white on the sides of his head, his wrinkled-face smiling at the sight of young Larry, "Master Larry.." the Butler nodded as the boy and his Father entered the home, "Sir.." the Butler nodded and addressed the boys Father, as he watched the two enter, and begin removing their wet coats to hand to the man who greeted them.

"George.." Lawrence replied with a nod, as he handed the Butler his coat, "Are the others here yet?" he asked, watching as Larry removed his coat, and handed it to the Butler as well.

The Butler nodded as he closed the door, took the coats, and pointed to the large staircase in front of them, "Ye'sir.." he replied with a nod, "They be waitin' fer you in the bedroom.." he said in his accent.

Lawrence nodded, and looked at the large staircase before him, sighed, and began walking slowly to the steps, "Larry.." he said over his shoulder, and watched as his son followed.

As the pair walked up the carpeted steps, voices could be heard from the right, as well as laughter from the left. Reaching the stairs, Lawrence instructed his son to find his cousins, and join them in the bedroom. Getting to the top of the stairs, Larry went left, and watched as his Father solemnly went right. Larry went to the end bedroom, gathered his two cousins, and led them to the bedroom of his Grandfather Bernard.

Larry had two cousins, Jimmy and Helen, who were siblings. Jimmy was three years older than Larry, while Helen was only a few months younger than Larry. While Larry and Helen were close, and friends, Jimmy was slightly hardened by his ego, and was led to believe he would be the one to take over the Family Business.

As the three children entered the darkened room, lit only by a few candles, and a small bedside lamp with a green shade, they saw their Grandfather lying in his bed, looking weathered and frail, covered to his chest with a blue blanket, and wires protruding beneath the blanket attached to the machines that beeped and whirled next to his bed. The three stopped between their respective father's, and starred at the dying old man before them.

Standing around the bed was the children of Bernard, his two sons, Lawrence and his slightly older brother, Jake, and their three sisters, Mary, Elizabeth, and Susan, all of which were not married, nor bore any children for the family lineage. Their jobs within the family and business were not what they had wished or wanted, but Bernard had made it clear they would never be involved in anything more than spending the money the family made, and teaching the World the cruel lessons it had deserved for generations.

The three children listened to the adults talk the family business with their dying Grandfather, as they looked at each other, and wondered why each of them was standing there in the dark room. Without warning, they would quickly find out.

"Jake.." Bernard said in his raspy-death voice, ".. I have watched you almost make a mockery of your life, teaching that, 'boy' of yours, 'cough, cough'.." he choked as he wiped his mouth, "that fucking brat of yours, the shit he shouldn't do, or treat people.." he said, looking at Jimmy with a scowl, "and its too late to whoop his ass with some morals.." he said as he peered at the older cousin of Larry.

Jake looked at Lawrence, then his son, and at Bernard, "But, Pops.." he started, and was stopped.

Bernard raised his hand to stop Jake's response, "Shut it.." he said, looking at Jimmy again, then at Jake, "I watched that kid of yours hit the dog with a shovel, push the maid down the stairs, and treat his own sister like she was less than human.." he scalded, looking back at Jimmy, "and if you were my son, and not my grandson, I would have kicked your ass long ago" he said, turning his attention back to Jake, "as I should have done with you" he scoffed.

Jake and Jimmy stood there with their brows furrowing, their faces turning red, as their future with the family and leadership ending before their eyes.

Bernard looked at Lawrence, and Larry, and forced a smile, "It's yours now, Lawrence, and Larry.." he said as he pointed at a man in a suit sitting in the corner of the room in the dark, "Mr. Cohen has papers for you to sign, and then it's yours.." he said with pride.

Jake looked at his younger brother, then at his dad, "Pops! You cant be fucking serious!" he demanded, then looked at Larry, "and him!? You are leaving this to him!?" he asked angrily, in almost disbelief.

Bernard looked at Jake, then at Larry, and smiled, "At least I know it wont go to shit" he chuckled, and smiled at Larry, "take it all in, learn, and no matter what Larry, learn to love.." he said as he closed his eyes for a moment.

Mr. Cohen withdrew a folder from his briefcase next to his feet, rose from his chair, and walked slowly to Lawrence and Larry, handing Lawrence the folder and a pen, "Second page.." he said sweetly, looking down at Larry and smiling. Lawrence signed, and handed the folder and pen back to Mr. Cohen, who leaned down, handed the pen to Larry, and smiled as he turned the page, and to a line at the bottom, "gimme your best Larry writing right there.." he said, and watched Larry scribble his name as only a seven-year-old could, "Perfect.." he said, standing, closing the folder, and returning to his chair slowly.

Jimmy looked at his cousin Larry, frowned, and then at his sister with a look of disgust, before turning and leaving the bedroom in a huff, as he ran away from the bedroom, down the stairs, and out of the house into the rain.

Bernard watched the tantrum of the older cousin, shook his head, and motioned for Larry to approached the bed, "Come, Larry.." he said softly as he reached under his blanket slowly as if searching for something, withdrew his hand as a fist, and held it out for the young boy as he approached his ailing-Grandfather.

Larry walked slowly, looking at the closed fist, then up to his smiling and weakened Grandfather, stopping by the bed, and looking at the fist again.

Bernard rotated his closed fist, and opened it slowly, revealing a coin, "This, represents the power we, this family, has over the people of this Nation.." he began as the boy peered into the palm, starring at the coin, "the... control.. our family has had through time.." he stated as he closed his eyes to recall some memories, teachings, and lessons passed down to him, "and the, the power, we will always have, as long as you hold true the meaning behind this.." he said as he opened his eyes, looking into the eyes of the young boy, and offering the coin to Larry.

Larry slowly reached out to the open palm, gently taking the coin from the frail hand, and looking at it.

"That was given to me by my Grandfather, when I was about your age" Bernard cooed gently, a smile growing across his face slowly.

Larry looked at the date, "18..71..?" he asked, looking up at his father, Lawrence, then at Bernard.

"Compassion, Larry.." Bernard said with a nod, as he looked at Helen with a smile, then back at Larry, "And the women of this family, are not weak, Larry.." he said, looking at his daughters with a look of sadness, "And I am sorry, so sorry, it took me this long to realize that.." he said, closing his eyes, and leaning his head back to rest on the pillow.

Larry looked at Helen, then at his Aunt's, down to the coin, and thought about his cousin, Jimmy, and the tantrum that had just occurred, "Yes, Grandfather.." he said, looking at the old man in his bed, head leaned back, as the machines that beeped, stopped, and releasing a steady tone of death.

Larry took that lesson to heart for several years of his childhood, embracing his cousin Helen as if she would one day help him lead the family. But sadly, that embrace, would end with her death at the hands of her brother, Jimmy, on her sixteenth birthday, forever altering Larry, his heart, compassion, and will to see anything other than what humanity was; Jealous.

A week after the funeral for Helen, Larry found Jimmy, and fed him to the boar that roamed the countryside. With his life altered, his views of humanity stained, Larry hardened his heart, and began to treat people as he knew he shouldn't, as the 'Sheep' his cousin Jimmy said they were. After that, Larry would never allow his heart get involved, and his compassion would be for himself, always.

There was a knock on the large double-doors to Larry's office, as the old man finished typing the last few words on his keyboard, paused, and reached for his blue coffee cup on his right side, "Yeah?" he said loudly, and watched as the door opened.

A beautiful Redhead pushed the door open, and greeted her boss with a grin, "She is here, Sir" she stated, her long legs protruding towards the ground from her short, pink skirt, as her pink blouse hugged her slender and tight body, accentuating her large breasts.

Larry admired his Secretary for a moment, set his cup down, and leaned back, "Show her in" he said as he exhaled, almost irritated he was being bothered.

A moment later, Roxie walked past the Secretary with a nod, and stopped just clear of the double-doors.

"That will be all Maria, thank you" Larry said to his Secretary with a nod, and received one in return as the door closed, leaving Larry and Roxie alone in the large room, "That was a good tip you gave me" he said, opening the desk drawer to his right, and pulling a thick, white envelope from the drawer, tossing it on the desk and watching it slide to the opposite end towards Roxie.

Roxie's eyes widened at the thick-offer as it slid towards her, then towards Larry, "Thank you, sir" she said nervously as she stood there trying not to shake.

"Please, have a seat" Larry said as he offered the large chair near the envelope, and reached for his cup again.

Roxie paused for a moment, swallowed hard, and walked slowly towards her chair. She began thinking of the day she had met the man on the other side of the desk, the promises of wealth and life he offered, and also the threats he mad if she would betray him after the offer. She could feel her body warming, as her armpits began to moisten under her arms and white button-up blouse as she took her seat, smoothed her blouse and skirt, and placed her hands in her lap, as she moved her attention to the envelope, and back to Larry.

Larry set his cup down again, cleared his throat, smirked at Roxie, and leaned forward to place his elbows on the edge of the desk, clasping his hands, and resting his mouth on the clasped fists, "Does Leticia suspect anything?" he asked as he spoke through his clasped hands.

Roxie thought of the question for a moment, and shook her head, "No, sir.." she said sweetly, her face emotionless.

Larry nodded slightly and lowered his hands a few inches below his chin, exposing his mouth, "And that cousin of yours?" he asked, a little more concerned.

Again, Roxie shook her head, "No, sir.." she said a little more direct, looking at the envelope again, then back at Larry.

Larry removed his arms from the edge of the desk, leaned back in his chair, and looked to his left out the large windows to his office as they were more than one-hundred floors above the New York skyline, with the Statue of Liberty in the distance, "I want Leticia's head.." he said sternly as he starred out the window, his voice as serious as he could be, turning his attention to the envelope, and then to Roxie as he looked her in her scared eyes, "bring that to me, and there will no end to those envelopes" he said as he leaned forward a little, and pushed the envelope closer to Roxie.

Roxie's eyes widened at the offer, and opportunity, leaned forward to accept the envelope, gently opened it, and saw three-bands of ten-thousands dollars each, and gasped, "Th-thank you, sir" she said as she closed the envelope, and placed it in her lap.

Larry nodded and leaned back again, "What would you really like, Roxie? What would be the dream of dreams you would want?" he asked, reaching for his cup again, and bringing it to his lips to await her answer.

Roxie placed her hands on the envelope, tapped it a few times to allow her mind to wander and think, and smiled when she knew what she wanted, "Hawaii.." she said matter-of-factly as she stopped tapping her fingers on the envelope in her lap.

Larry stopped drinking from his cup, lowered it and set it on the table, and smiled as he nodded to the envelope, "Don't spend that all at once, or deposit any of it, understood?" he reminded her.

Roxie nodded in agreement, "I remember, sir" she said as she placed her hand on the envelope, "I'll stick this one with the others I have, for a rainy day" she smirked as she stood, "And thank you, sir, for the opportunity.." she said as she waited for him to dismiss her.

Larry nodded, and gave her a wave of his left hand to dismiss her, reached for his coffee, and watched Roxie turn and walk away, admiring her tight rear swaying side to side as she left the room as he took a sip, and watched the door open, and close to his office. As he set the cup down, he paused, and pushed the intercom on his phone to his Secretary, "Maria, can I see you please?" he asked as nice as he could.

A moment later, the door to his office opened again, and the Redhead appeared in her pink outfit once again, and smiled, "Sir?" she asked as the door shut behind her, and took a step inside the room.

Larry stood and walked to the large, thick windows in his office, and peered out to look at the people below, "Is she still single?" he asked, not turning his head.

Maria thought for a moment, "Yes, sir" she replied, "I don't think she trusts anyone enough to let them in, especially while she is working for you" she said as a best-guess.

Larry nodded and smiled, turning to look at Maria, "Maybe, we can fix that.." he said matter-of-factly as he winked at his Secretary.

Maria nodded and smirked, "Understood, sir" she replied, and paused, "Male, or female?" she asked just to be clear.

Larry chuckled to himself as he looked out the window, folding his arms across his chest to ponder for a moment, "Both" he said with a hint of mischievousness in his voice at the thought of Roxie being a 'Chinese finger trap' between two lovers, and listened as the door to his office opened, and closed behind his beautiful Secretary.

Chapter 8

With the first two years of Leticia's second term completed, and the Country seemingly healed from the Stock Market Crash that nearly crippled its economy, the President knew that her People deserved more, and wanted to give it to them. The potential 'crash' that Larry had begun had rippling effects across many countries and

Nations, and while there were many Leticia could not help, there were two that she could; Canada and Mexico.

Leticia had sent her Agent in White, and the Agent in Yellow with the Pink tie to deliver a message in person to both leaders of those two countries to come to Washington D.C. for a small, and secret conference, with a surprise Leader no one would see coming.

Arriving back in D.C., the Agent in White escorted the two Leaders across the lawn from the landing helicopter, through the large doors of the White House, down the busy halls of tourists and workers, and waited outside the main doors to the Oval Office as Roxie sat at her desk and smiled at the two leaders, and Agent.

"Was it a safe flight?" Roxie asked the two Leaders with a smile.

The Leaders looked at the Secretary with a smile, as the Agent in White turned their attention to the Secretary, and shook their head side to side, as if too stop the interaction before it started, and pointed to the phone for Roxie to notify the President the Guests were there, and watched as Roxie's attitude changed as she did her job.

Roxie picked up the phone, pressed one button, and waited a moment, "Madam President, your Guests are here" she said without any emotion, paused, and hung up the phone, "She's ready for you" she said sternly as she looked at the Agent in White with a slight glare.

The Agent in White nodded, stepped towards the door, turned the knob, pushed the door open and stepped through and to the side, and watched as the Leaders entered the room. The Agent in White closed the door, and looked at Roxie as the door closed.

Leticia stood from her desk, smiled, and walked to the two Leaders with her hand out as she greeted them, "President Colon.." she said, shaking the hand of the President of Mexico, and looking at the other Man, "Prime Minister Morin.." she said, shaking the hand of the Leader of Canada, "Please, have a seat" she said, offering her office and chairs to her guests, and nodded to the Agent in White, and watched as the Agent walked to the other side-door, knocked twice, and opened it.

The Agent in White nodded inside the room, and stood back to wait, as an Olive-skinned Man in a dark suit approached, wearing elaborate necklaces full of colors and turquoise, beautiful wrist bands that matched, and two long braids that protruded from the back of the Man's head, draped over his shoulders, down his chest that reached his waist.

Leticia smiled at the Man as he walked through the door as the Agent in White closed the door behind him, and stepped to the side to stand next to the American flag, and wait.

"President Colon, Prime Minister Morin" Leticia said as she turned her attention to the Man in the elaborate attire, "Can I introduce to you the Leader of the Native Nation, Chief Dancing Bear.." she said as the Chief entered the room, nodded with a smiled, approached the two Men, shook hands, and sat across from them with a nod.

Leticia sat in the empty chair next to the Chief, "Would anyone like some coffee, tea, water?" she asked her guests, and was graciously turned down.

"Really curious as to why you brought us here, Madam President" President Colon said with a thick accent, as he moved to the end of his seat, and leaned forward to rest his elbows on his knees and show his time was precious.

"Agreed" Prime Minister Morin said as he leaned back, set his elbow on the arm of the chair, and rested his head against his fist.

Leticia looked at the Chief, who nodded with a smile, and turned her attention back to the other two Men, "We, want to save your countries, and unite us.." she said bluntly, as she too sat back in her chair, and let the sentence swirl in the heads of her two guests.

The PM and President looked at each other for a moment, then at the Chief, and turned their attention back to Leticia, "Excuse me?" the PM said as he sat straight up in his chair, and lowered his arm to his lap.

Leticia stood and walked to her desk, retrieving several folders, and walked back to her seat next to the Chief, "As you both know, the Stock Market crash nearly crippled this country.." she said as she handed each of the

Leaders a folder, and sat in her chair again, "and, as you also know, I brought this Country back from that brink, and are now slowly, once again, rebuilding this Nation as to what it once was" she said as she watched the Leaders open their folders, and begin reading the reports, "but, I.." she said and paused as she looked at Chief Dancing Bear, "excuse me, We.." she said with a smile as she corrected herself, "We, know what that crash also did to both of your countries" she said, and paused as she gave the two men across from her a chance to read the first page.

The PM and President of Mexico read down the page, their eyes widening at what they read, and as they got to the bottom of the page, paused, and looked at each other, "Is this for real?" the President of Mexico asked as he looked at the page again.

Leticia nodded and smiled, "More than real" she said as she looked at Chief Dancing Bear, "We, have the means, to not only unite us as One Nation, while eliminating the Cartels that are devastating your streets and peoples.." she said to President Colon, "but also boosting your economy, and health care.." she added, and watched President Colon turn the page to read on, "as well as the Indigenous Rights of your People, Prime Minister.." she said, looking at PM Morin.

The PM looked at Leticia, then at Chief Dancing Bear who was glaring at the PM with intent, and then back at the page in front of him, as he too turned to look at the second page, and paused, "A, 'Super.. Nation..?" the PM asked as he looked up at Leticia and the Chief.

Chief Dancing Bear smiled and nodded, "You, should keep reading Prime Minister" he suggested in a deep tone that demanded the respect and attention his voice deserved.

The PM didn't hesitate, and read on as Leticia spoke.

"I am not the one in charge fella's" Leticia chuckled as she watched her two guests read the second page, "We, the four of us, will be, for the better of our lands and peoples" she said as she sat back a little, and looked at the Agent in White, held up her hand, and watched as the Agent walked to the main door of the Oval Office, opened it, and disappeared closing the door behind them, "Think of the possibilities of our combined Militaries, the ways in which we could really, and truly help each other with health care, a common currency, and to eliminate the Cartels that are literally destroying your country" she said to President Colon.

The PM stopped reading, and looked at Leticia, "You want us to unite the three Nations?" he asked with a hint of doubt in his voice.

"Four, Nations" Chief Dancing Bear corrected with a smile.

Prime Minister Morin looked at the Chief quickly, then back to Leticia, "Sorry, Four Nations.." he corrected, shaking his head, "and, why would we agree to any of this?" he asked, looking at the President next to him who was still reading.

President Colon stopped reading, and looked up, "I'm in.." he said without hesitation, closing his folder, and tossing it on the table between them, leaning back, smiling, and nodding to Chief Dancing Bear.

Prime Minister Morin looked on in shock to the Mexican President, "Are you fucking crazy?!" he demanded, "Did you see what you are giving up?" he asked as he looked back at the pages before him, "Half your land goes back to the Native Tribes, fifteen percent of your economy goes back to the Native Tribes, and you are okay with that?" he asked in a tone of frustration.

President Colon laughed at the Prime Minister as he looked at him, "And did you see how safe my Country and its people would be? The growth of the economy over the first ten years alone!?" he said with a chuckle, "And to be rid of those fucking animals that make my countrymen and women live in fear of walking their own streets! It is not even a question! Yes, I am in!" he demanded to the PM, and nodded to Chief Dancing Bear and Leticia.

Prime Minister Morin closed his folder, and shook his head, "My country will never go for this" he said as he too tossed the folder on the table, and looked up as the Agent in White reentered the room carrying a tray with glasses and four bottles of alcohol; Tequila, Whiskey, Vodka, and Wine.

Chief Dancing Bear inched forward slowly in his chair, leaned forward, and looked right at the PM, "What, do you have against equality?" he asked, and waited.

The Agent in White paused as the question was asked, looked at the Prime Minister, and continued to the table between the four Leaders, set the tray down, and walked back to the spot next to the Flag, and waited.

Prime Minister Morin let the question swirl in his head for a moment, and thought about the backlash he, and his country, had received over the last forty-years for their inhuman treatment of the Indigenous People of his Country, the mass murders of the past, and the continued mistreatment of the Women of his country, "I, I..." he stammered, and looked at President Colon.

"Don't look at me, Pinche" President Colon said with a chuckle, "Your whole country is filled with pendejo's.." he laughed as he looked at the bottle of Tequila on the table before him, and smiled there was no lime or salt.

Morin looked at Colon with a scowl, then back to Leticia who was staring back at him with a soft look, and for an answer as well.

The Prime Minister stood from his chair slowly, and looked down at the bottle of Whiskey his country produced, and walked behind his chair, stopping, and looking at the Chief, "My grandparents were.." he began, and was interrupted.

"Are you your grandparents?" Chief Dancing Bear asked boldly as he looked up at the towering PM as he stood behind his chair, "Because if not, you, Prime Minister, are being given the chance to fix a problem that has plagued your Nation for generations, to give Hope, and Peace, to a People that has known nothing but hatred for a Land they occupied way before those Colonizers came with their diseases, empty and false promises, and destroyed the homes of those before" he said as he too looked at the tray on the table, and smiled at the wine, "That is a great choice, Madam President" he said with a smile and nod.

The Prime Minister looked over his shoulder at the Agent in White for a few moments, "Do, we each get our own protective force of them?" he asked as he turned his attention back to Leticia as he leaned forward and placed his hands on the top of the chair he sat in a moment ago.

Leticia and the Chief looked at each other for a moment, and smiled, "They are a standard issue, yes" she said as she leaned back in her chair gently, feeling as though she was making a breakthrough.

Prime Minister Morin thought for a moment, and slowly walked around his chair, and sat once more, looking at the other Leaders, and nodded, "And, we all have a say in how this, 'Super Nation', is run?" he asked, looking for reassurance that he, and his country, would not be hung out to dry.

Leticia smiled as she scooted forward in her chair, leaned towards the tray of alcohol, and began pouring the Whiskey into a glass, "Yes.." she said, replacing the top on the Whiskey bottle, and reaching for the Tequila.

Prime Minister Morin took the answer, and thought for a moment as he watched the President of the Current United States, pour Tequila into a glass and replace the top, pour Wine into a glass, and replace the cork, and unscrew the top to the Vodka, then paused as she looked up at the Prime Minister.

Prime Minister Morin nodded a few times as he thought, and looked at Chief Dancing Bear, "I am willing to try" he said, and watched as Leticia poured the Vodka into the last glass, replaced the lid, and leaned back.

Chief Dancing Bear nodded and smiled, "All we can do, Prime Minister, is try" he said as he leaned forward and took his glass of Wine, and held it up to the man across from him.

The three other Leaders reached for their respective glasses, held them up to toast to a new beginning, clinked the glasses, and sipped in unison.

Leticia smiled as she lowered her glass, "We know this will take time, right?" she asked as she looked at the three men with her, "and I don't think I need to say how hush-hush this is at this time, right?" she asked as she watched the three men lower their glasses from their lips, and nod, and while I don't intend to seek a third term in office, I would like to solidify this before the elections, and have a Unified Celebration within the next eighteen months" she said as she looked at the Men and waited for a reply.

The three Leaders nodded in unison as they each took another sip, and watched as the Agent in White walked towards the door to leave once more.

The Prime Minister watched the Agent leave the room, and looked at Leticia for a moment, "You know, there are many who are comparing you, and your antics, to that of Hitler, right?" he asked as he took another sip of his Whiskey, and lowered his arm with the glass to rest on the arm of his chair.

Leticia paused at the comment, and chuckled, "I, am aware, yes" she said as she set her glass on the tray, and leaned back, "But, none of them are saying it to my face" she said with a chuckle as she looked at the other two men, "and if you look at what has been done for the People, what would you compare me too?" she asked, waiting for a reply.

Before the Prime Minister could answer, the door to the Oval Office opened once more, and the Agent in

White stood waiting with several other Agents in Yellow suits and black ties.

"Thank you, Gentleman, for coming" Leticia said as she stood from her chair, and began walking to her desk, "the Agents will escort you home, safely, and I look forward to joining these Nations together in the months to come" she finished, as she sat behind her desk, and watched as each of her guests finished their drinks in a quick swallow, stood, smiled and nodded to their Hostess, and followed the Agents from the Office, with the door closing behind them, with the Agent in White staying behind, "You, think I'm a lot like Hitler?" she asked the Agent at the door.

The Agent in White paused, then shook their head back and forth.

Leticia thought for a moment at her own heritage, the struggles her family had gone through for the last hundred years, and hoped she was able to help those of the future, escape the hatred and persecution of the past. She looked at the tray on the coffee table she was just at, the four different alcohols that were shared, and smiled at the potential that could be, as she looked at the Agent in White, smiled, and dismissed with the wave of a hand.

Several moments later, the phone rang on Leticia's desk, as a light was flashing, and she smiled as she answered it, "Hey Sundae" she said with a chuckle, "Yeah, yeah, he was the reluctant one, you were right" she laughed as she leaned back in her large chair, "Okay, yeah, we can start to plan that.." she said and paused, "but that's why we keep this as close to the chest as possible, if Larry was to find out about this before we have a chance to set things in motion?" she said and paused again, "Exactly, but I have a few things in the works to flush the.. yeah.. yeah.. publicly.." said and laughed, "okay Sundae, yeah, see ya soon for drinks, and yes, he will be there" she said mysteriously and laughed as she hung up the phone, spun in her chair to gaze out the Oval Office window, and watched as the Presidential helicopter lifted off the ground, taking her guests back to the airport, and the new idea of a 'Super Country' and its hopes and dreams, lifting off with it.

Chapter 9

Over the next few months, Leticia and the new Leaders met in secret several times to discuss new laws and procedures that would not only benefit, but protect, the citizens of the new Country that would soon be unveiled to the world, one question kept arising that stumped and wondered the four as they met; What would the new Country be called. As the four jotted down idea after idea over those months, there was one that seemed to not only define what they were trying to accomplish, but gave pride and distinction to that idea.

The United Nation of Nations would unite Canada, America, The Indigenous Nations, and Mexico, and eliminate any border that would try to separate any of them. The wall that had been built by the hatred of one of the previous Presidents would be torn down and hauled into the sea, and would be just a memory as that of the one that separated Germany until the nineteen-eighties. And while each Leader would remain in their own Government Building they previously occupied, none would have more power than the next.

Just before the Fourth of July, months after the meeting, Leticia met with Holly, and Sundae, to discuss how the executions would process once the new Country was established. As the three women sat in the Oval Office, Leticia noticed Holly was quite removed from the conversation.

"You okay Holly?" Leticia asked to her Executioner as the large-hipped woman sat solemn in her chair, barely talking, and obviously preoccupied with other thoughts.

Holly starred at the words on the pages before her, and looked up slowly, "I, I cant do this anymore" she said, her voice low and sad.

Sundae looked at Leticia with a saddened eyes, then at Holly, "What's going on, Holly?" she asked, setting her notebook on the table between them, as she crossed her left leg over her right, and gave her friend the attention Holly deserved.

Holly didn't raise her head as she peered at the page before her, "I, I.. cant pretend that executing my niece didn't alter me at all" she stammered as she fought back tears, her voice quaking slightly as a tear fell to the page below her face, "my nephew hates me, and wont talk to me" she said sadly as she reached up and wiped her eyes with her thumb, "my sister wont talk to me, and my family has all but ostracized me from any activity and holiday.." she continued, her voice cracking slightly as the sadness filled the room.

Sundae looked at Leticia again, and while her eyes and face turned red and sad as well, she fought back the tears Holly seemed to release, turning her attention back to Holly, "Do, you need to take a break? A vacation?" she asked, holding her composure the best she could, the emotions filling the room and effecting the Women in charge.

Holly shook her still lowered head, pulled her gun from the holster on her large hip, and set it on the table, "I'm, done.." she said sadly as she released the gun, placing her hand on her blue-dressed lap, and closed her eyes.

Leticia watched her friend for a moment, and could feel the weight Holly was carrying, "I never even thought to ask how this was effecting you, of any of it.." she said caringly, looking from the gun on that table that had taken more lives in the name of 'Justice', to her friend who carried the burdens of the souls she had taken, "and I have to take a lot of that pain and guilt as well" she said, hoping her words would comfort Holly in some way.

Holly listened for a moment, and looked at Leticia, her eyes swollen and red as they dripped the tears for all the lives and families she had taken and altered, "I can understand why Jake took his life after he realized he killed his own son.." she said as she fought back the tears that wanted to pour, "and do you know, how many nights over the last year I have sat at home, placed that barrel in my mouth, and wanted to pull that trigger? You know how many nights, I have removed that barrel, and drowned my thoughts in a bottle?" she asked as the emotion fell from her lips.

Sundae looked at Leticia as she listened to the pain, her head shaking slowly at the news that their 'strongest' member, had lost her heart.

Leticia looked at Sundae, then at Holly again, "What, what can we do, Holly?" she asked, hoping she could ease the pain of her friend.

Holly wiped her eyes, and stood, removing the gun belt from around her thick waist, and setting it on the seat she just occupied, "Let me go home, and don't ever call me again.." she said, her blue dress slightly swaying as she moved to drop the belt, and looked at the President, "Just, leave me alone, please..?" she asked, and without permission, turned and began walking to the door of the Oval Office.

Sundae and Leticia watched their friend depart their sitting area and head to the door, and stop.

Holly stopped just before the door, lowered her head for a moment, raised it again, and turned to look at Leticia, "You have some great ideas, Leticia, some amazing ideas" she said as the tears slowly rolled down her round cheeks, "but remember, Hitler had some amazing ideas to unite his country and people too, and what happened to him?" she asked, and paused, "What happened to the country he tried to build, the ideas he tried to implement, and the hearts of hatred that destroyed a race of people?" she asked as she watched her questions impact the woman that was trying to 'save' a Nation, "And, if you are not careful, Letty, what will the history books say about you when this is all done? You have less than eighteen months left in Office before the People elect new Leaders of this Country you brought back from the brink of anarchy.." she said as she reached blindly for the door knob next to her, "are you proud of what you have accomplished with all the death and blood on your hands?" she asked, and watched the women before her stare back at her with saddened eyes.

Leticia let the questions bombard her ears, and swirl in her brain as she looked at her friend about to walk from her life forever.

Holly forced a smile through her tears, turned the knob in her hand, pulled the door, and left the Office leaving the door open as she walked past the desk of Roxie, "Take care, Rox.." she said as she walked slowly, turned left, and disappeared from sight of the women in the Office.

Leticia looked at Sundae, then at Roxie who was staring back in the Office at her Boss with a confused look. Sundae stood and walked to the door, nodded to Roxie, closed the door, and walked back to the sitting area, and stopped behind the chair opposite Leticia.

"You, okay, Letty?" Sundae asked as she set her hands on the back of the chair to brace herself.

Leticia starred at the door, then looked at Sundae, and slowly shook her head, "No, I don't think so Sundae, no.." she said, standing and slowly walking to the window, her mind racing with the departure of her friend, and the questions hanging over her head.

Sundae was at a loss of words for a moment, "Is there, anything I can do?" she asked, letting go of the chair, and standing tall, trying to be strong for them both.

Leticia slightly shook her head as she peered out the window, "Yeah.." she said as she fought back tears, "take over for a week, I'm going to the Vineyard for a few days, have the Agent meet me there, please..” she said in a weakened voice.

Sundae nodded, “Yes, Ma’am” she replied, paused to wait further instructions, and when there was none, turned to walk to the door to leave.

“And Sundae?” Leticia said softly as she turned from the window to look at her Vice President.

Sundae stopped and turned, looking at Leticia, “Yes, Ma’am?” she asked soothingly.

“Find that fucking mole, will you?” Leticia said sternly, trying to snap herself from her saddened mood.

Sundae nodded and forced a slight smile, “Yes Ma’am” she replied with a nod, and turned to leave the Office, opening the door, and walking past Roxie as she left the door open.

Roxie looked in the Office for a moment, rose from her desk, and stood at the entrance to the Office, “Ma’am, is there anything I can do?” she asked, reaching for the door knob to close it.

Leticia looked at the blonde Secretary, "Make arrangements for the Vineyard, please, I want to leave within the hour" she ordered as she turned to walk to her desk.

Roxie nodded, "Anything else, Ma'am?" she asked as she pulled the door slowly towards her.

Leticia shook her head, "No, Rox, that will be all, thank you" she said as she reached her seat, pulled the chair, and sat.

Roxie nodded, and pulled the door closed behind her.

Leticia sat at her desk, and looked at her phone for a moment. She had so many questions she realized would never be answered, and while she didn't have many she could talk too to help ease her pain and burdens, there was one that would always tell her what she needed to hear. She picked up her phone, pressed some numbers, and waited as the phone rang on the other end.

"Hello?" came a sweet voice on the other end.

"Mom?" Leticia sounded as her voice cracked from the turmoil of her morning, "Do you have a minute?" she asked, and began to pour her heart out to the woman that bore her.

Arriving later that evening at the Vineyard, Leticia walked through the large home towards her bedroom, and tossed her purse and small bag on the bed. She would be having several guests join her within the next few hours, but the time alone would be needed to gather her composure and get her emotions and thoughts in order. As she sat on the corner of the bed, there was a slight knock at her opened bedroom door, turning to look, it was the Agent in White standing there, holding a small book, and waiting for further instructions.

"Is, that from my Mom?" Leticia asked as she looked at the small book.

The Agent nodded, and held the book out.

Leticia held out her hand, "Please?" she asked, and watched the Agent enter her room, and walk towards her slowly, handing her the small book, and turning to leave without orders, and pausing at the door when the President spoke again, "Are you, happy?" she asked as she held the book in her hands, and looked at the Agent as they stopped.

The Agent turned to look in the direction of the President, nodded slightly, and turned to leave again.

Leticia watched the Agent leave, and looked down at the small book again in her hands, and read the word on the front 'Dziennik', which meant 'Diary' in Polish, and below the word, was the Jewish star. Leticia sat puzzled for a moment, opened it, and began to read the entries of the woman she called Abuela, Grandmother in Spanish.

For her whole life, Leticia had been told her lineage was from Mexico, that they could trace their roots back to the Aztecs, that her family had been pioneers of the founding of Mexico, and as she read the first few pages, she realized her whole life was a lie. Her Grandmother, and Great Grandmother, had escaped the camps in Poland on a small boat to Argentina in the early nineteen-forties, and made their way to Mexico over the next few years, learning the language as they went, and forgetting their heritage so they could blend into their new lives as Mexicans. Their skin was similar already, and while they would need to learn a whole new culture and way of life to hide who they once were, the survivors knew it was for their own safety.

Her Grandmother had changed her name from Alicja, to Alicia in her new homeland, and while they were marked with the numbers of the Reich, they burned the marks off with heated metal and made excuses as to why the scars were there, fading over time as they worked in the Southern hemispheric sun. Over the years, Alicia had perfected her dialect, got an education, and met a man that would give her a family. As Leticia read, the tears fell from her eyes to the diary in her hands, and she realized that while she wasn't marking her citizens with tattooed numbers on their forearms, she was causing many of her Citizens the same pains and traumas as the man who forced her family to flee their homes nearly one-hundred years prior, and she hated herself for it.

The more Leticia read about her Grandmothers life, the more she understood why the information had been hidden from her, and the world, and what would happen if the information ever got out. She thought about what her mother had been through, the secrets and burdens she carried about the history, and her mind once more went to the questions Holly had asked in the Office that morning. Leticia closed the book, placed it next to her, rose from the edge of the bed, and walked into the bathroom to mourn the life she would never know.

Leticia showered, got dressed in a blue track suit, with red sneakers, and left her bedroom to head to the main room of the large home at the Vineyard, and await her guests who would be arriving shortly. As she walked into the living room, she heard noises coming from the kitchen, and proceeded to investigate the sounds. Entering the kitchen area, she saw the Agent in White preparing snacks for the guests, as she smiled at the sight of the one that made her feel safe.

"They will be here in a few minutes" Leticia said as she watched the Agent finish setting the snacks on the tray.

The Agent nodded without looking up.

"I take it, you heard about Holly?" she asked, her voice trying to be strong through the sad news.

The Agent paused for a second, nodded, and finished placing the last of the snacks on the tray, before looking in the direction of the President.

Leticia nodded, "Please, keep an eye on her for me, will ya?" she asked, and watched as the Agent nodded, picked up the tray, and left the kitchen to take the snacks to the conference room. Leticia followed behind slowly, keeping her distance for a moment, and could hear the large helicopter approaching, "Can you make sure the drinks are ready too, please?" she asked.

The Agent nodded, and disappeared through a door for a moment, and reappeared with another tray of glasses and ice, and pointed to the small bar near the door she had walked through.

Leticia chuckled and shook her head, "Is there anything you don't know?" she asked rhetorically.

The Agent nodded, and held up a finger.

Leticia paused, "The mole, right?" she asked, and watched as the Agent nodded, and held up a hand as if to say, 'just wait, I'll figure it out', and for a moment, Leticia was calm.

A few moments later, the main door opened, and the voices of her guests could be heard laughing as they entered the large home, "But you called my people pendejos!" the Prime Minister said with a laugh, "you know I had to look that up!?" he demanded with another laugh.

"Because they are" President Colon laughed as he entered the conference room, and saw Leticia, "Madam President" he said as he smiled, and tried to change the subject.

"Gentleman" Leticia said as she took a few steps to greet her guests, "And where, is Chief Dancing Bear?" she asked, looking past President Colon and the Prime Minister.

"He's coming" the Prime Minister said with a smile.

Leticia waited another moment, and could hear footsteps approaching again. Seconds later, Chief Dancing Bear entered the room carrying a large wooden box that had beautiful carvings of fish circling it, and setting it on the table near the tray of glasses and ice.

As the Four Leaders looked at the large wooden box in amazement and wonder, a cellphone rang in the pocket of the Agent, who pulled the phone from a pocket in the white jacket, pushed the green button on the screen, and placed the phone to the side of their head, and paused. A moment later, lowered the phone to their side, and approached Leticia slowly, handing her the phone, and waiting.

Leticia looked at the phone, then the Agent, and placed the phone to her ear, "Hello?" she asked confused, listened for a moment, and dropped the phone in shock, "Hol...Holly, has..." she stammered as she reached for a the back of the nearest seat, pulling it, and sitting slowly, "Holly has been assassinated" she said in disbelief, as her guests looked on in confusion, and the Agent in White left the conference room quickly, running to the helicopter in the field, and leaving the Vineyard without warning.

Chapter 10

It had been several months since Holly's death, and while the Country was flourishing as Leticia, The President of the United States, had set in motion for the Citizens she swore to protect, there was whispers and rumors of Coups, take-overs, and threats to destroy the Country from within, and now that the 'Executioner' was gone, her reign was near its end. There was a mole she was trying to uncover, a devious man trying to destroy the legacy Leticia was trying to build and leave to her predecessor, as well as seemingly safe three other Nations from the brink of their own demises. With just a year left in her second, and final term of Office, she had work to do.

Leticia's right-hand person, the Agent in White, had taken a few tasks to heart; Find the mole, find Holly's killer, and stop a Coup before it could gain traction. There had been several Coup attempts in the history of the Nation, and none more famous than the 'March on Washington' in January 2021, which lead to many hating the country they lived in, as well as making that Government a laughing stock of the World. The Agent in White made it their mission to not let that happen again, and would die to protect the World in which they lived.

Leticia had let the journal she read of her Grandmother's escape from the Nazi-Invasion of her homeland Poland, and over the months, began looking at her own reforms, and laws, and began to doubt the validity of those laws, and the future effects it would have on the future, as well as the Ideas the future Rulers would have as to what could-be, or would-be, acceptable for the Country. She began to have regrets of her 'Reform Camp', Nulla Reditus, and like the Gitmo before, she decided to close the Island Reform, and repurpose it to Teach the Youth, rather than forced discipline that would lead to more deaths of those who refused to conform to society. There was a better way, and she would use any means possible to make it happen.

After Thanksgiving, Leticia invited the Leaders of the proposed 'Super Nation' to Washington D.C. to set the meeting to plan to inform the Countries, and the World, of the idea. The Leaders, Chief Dancing Bear, President Colon, and Prime Minister Morin, arrived at the Military base near the Nation's Capitol, boarded the Presidential helicopter, and lifted off towards their meeting with President Gonzales. With the Leaders in the air, another secret meeting was held in the Oval Office.

"What have you found?" Leticia asked the Agent in White, as Sundae Jones sat in a chair next to the large, wooden desk, looking at the Agent as they removed their headwear, exposing their face for the first time to the Vice President.

Removing the White fedora, face-shield, and white head covering, the long, red-braided beard fell from the chin, as a smile appeared, "It's worse than we could have thought" the Agent said, his face looking back and forth to the powerful women before him.

Sundae starred at the Agent for a moment, and looked at Leticia, "Worse?" she asked, her face contorting with confusion, "You really do keep things close to the chest, don't you?" she asked, and looked at the Agent again, "Does this have to do with the mole?" she asked, and waited for the Agent to reply.

The Agent nodded, and then slightly shook his head, "It goes deeper than that" he replied, and looked at Leticia, "Roxie, is the mole" he said, and withdrew five, thick, white envelopes, and placed them on the corner of the desk, "These were found in her apartment, along with files from Larry on the SCOTUS, several Cabinet Members, and the House Majority" he said, removing a flash-drive from his pocket, and setting it on the envelope.

Leticia and Sundae looked at the closed door to the Oval Office quickly, paused as their brows furrowed in anger and disgust, looked at the items on the corner of the desk, then at each other, and began shaking their heads.

"Could Moxie be involved as well?" Sundae asked quickly, turning her attention from Leticia to the Agent.

The Agent shook his head, "I looked into that, deeply" he began quickly in defense of his friend, "Phone records, emails, phone taps.." he listed, "I even moved into Roxie's building to monitor her happenings, and other Roxie dating a man and woman who were obviously using her, there has been no communication between the cousins other than that interaction in the War Room that day" he said, turning his attention back to Leticia, "SCOTUS and the House Majority are behind the Coup" he said bluntly, and waited.

Leticia's eyes widened quickly, as she shook her head, and leaned back in her chair, "Those mother fuckers..!" she erupted, slapping the arms of her large chair with her palms, "and are they gaining any support?" she asked, looking at Sundae and waiting for the Agents reply.

The Agent nodded slightly, "They are definitely being funded, and bribed" he replied, "and it seems promises are being made that can not actually be cashed in on" he said, looking at the envelopes, then at Sundae, "and there's a plot to have you kidnapped, and held for ransom" he said quickly, and paused.

Sunday looked at the Agent quickly, "What the fuck?" she blurted, "Why me?" she asked, placing her hand on her chest, and looking confused.

"Because of what, and who, you represent" the Agent replied, looking at Leticia, then out the window behind her as he heard, and watched, the helicopter land, "and, they are not safe, either" he said, pulling his head-covering back on his head, tucking his braided beard.

The Women looked at each other shaking their heads.

"What should I do about Roxie?" the Agent asked as he donned his White fedora, holding his face-visor in his right hand.

Leticia leaned forward and slid the envelopes and flash-drive towards her, opened the top drawer, and brushed the items in, closing the drawer, "We will discuss that after we are done with them.." she said as she turned and watched the Leaders exit the large helicopter, and slowly stroll across the lawn, smiling and laughing, "This unification is more important than her, me, either of you.." she said as she stood, and forced a smile, "We will deal with her, and Larry.." she said, her smile turning into a smirk.

The Agent smiled and nodded, placed the visor in his face to cover his identity once more, saluted the Women of Power, turned, and walked towards the door, pausing, and turning their head to look at the President.

Leticia nodded, kept her smile, and watched as the door opened, revealing Roxie sitting at her desk, typing away, oblivious to the meeting that had just happened, "And can you ask the Agent in Red to accompany you next time, please? As well as the Agent in Yellow, ya know, with the pink tie?" she asked, and watched as the Agent nodded, and left the Oval Office, passing the desk of Roxie, taking a left, and disappearing from sight.

Leticia nodded to Sundae, and smiled, "I have to say.." she said, just loudly enough for Roxie to hear, but quiet enough that the secretary would have to be listening intently, "I would not have thought the Minority Leader would be that conniving" she said with a wink and smirk.

Sundae held back her smile and slightly shook her head, "Are we going to let the Agents handle it?" she asked, fighting the urge to look and see if Roxie was listening.

Leticia nodded as she opened the drawer to her desk that held the envelopes the Agent in White had handed her, looked at the stack, closed the drawer, and looked at her VP again, "Most likely, but I will know more after this meeting" she said as she leaned forward, grabbing a pen, and scribbling a note on a piece of paper, tearing it from the small pad, folding it in half, and reaching it out for Sundae to take, "Let me know by Monday if this works for you, okay?" she asked with a smirk and a nod.

Sundae reached out and took the paper, opened it, read it quickly, folded it, and slid it in her pocket, "Yes, Ma'am" she said with a nod and a smile, "Will there be anything else?" she asked as the Women heard the Guests approaching the Oval Office.

Leticia shook her head, "No, Sundae, thank you, just close the door as you leave, okay?" she asked as she took a few steps from behind her desk to wait for her Guests.

"Yes, Ma'am" Sundae said, excusing herself towards the door, and standing to the side to allow the Guests to enter.

The three Leaders entered the Office, nodded and smiled to Sundae Jones as she stood and waited patiently for them to enter, and walk towards Leticia to greet her. As President Colon was the last to enter, Sundae nodded, and left the Office, closing the door behind her, leaving the meeting to happen behind closed doors.

"Gentleman, thank you for coming.." Leticia said sweetly as the men shook hands one at a time, and found a seat, "We have a lot to talk about, and not a lot of time, especially with Christmas right around the corner, and Elections happening in less than a year" she said, watching her Guests take a seat, and her sitting behind her desk once more in an official capacity, smiling, and folding her hands to place them gently on her desk.

Two months later, on January 11th, 2040, from an undisclosed location surrounded by trees and hills, the four Leaders of their Nations stood behind a long, wooden table made of Redwood from a fallen tree in Northern California, dressed in their best suits and regalia, and smiled into the camera as it panned slowly from left to right, zooming in to each face, and panning back to show the four as they seated at once. Slowly, Leticia stood from her seat, pushing the chair back with the back of her knees, and slowly walked to the podium.

Standing behind the podium, wearing a dark-purple dress, with yellow earrings, and white-pumps, and her hair done in a magnificent style, Leticia smiled at the small crowd of Dignitaries, and then into the camera, "My fellow Americans, Citizens of the Sovereign Nations, Canadians, and Citizens of the great country of Mexico.." she said as she smiled, turning her attention to the Leaders that sat not far from her, then back to the cameras, "Today, marks a great day in our history, as we.." she said as she spread her arms wide, "embark on a new journey of Unity, Peace, and Prosperity.." she said sweetly, a slight smile growing across her face as she gently nodded, looking down at her notes briefly, then back up to the cameras, "as we enter this new decade, not as four Nations divided by walls, tyranny, and currency, but to Unite, under one banner of equality, self-reliance, and determination for a brighter future, for our Citizens, YOU.." she said boldly with a proud smile, nodding to the cameras, then to her Guests sitting next to her, then back to the cameras, "For far too long, we have watched the struggles of our Neighbors to the South, struggle with violence, extreme-poverty, and an infestation of Cartels set to destroy because of greed.." she said, her tone turning more defensive and intolerable, "to our neighbors to the North, who continue to mistreat a majority of their Citizens based on gender, and race.." she said, a hint of sadness in her voice, as she paused for a moment, grabbing the sides of the podium, taking a step back to recompose herself, the stepping back to the podium, smiling gently, looking at her Guests once more with a nod, then back to the cameras, "and to the Great Sovereign Nation, that has had its lands stripped by the generations of Oppressors, Governments, and Genocides for their beliefs and lands.." she said sadly as she paused to let the cameras pan to the Guests at the table, and their solemn reaction to the speech being read and heard, "We say, No More!" she said, as the Guests stood proudly, taking each others hands, and holding them up, "Today, we Unite as One Nation, as One People, Under a Banner of Flags and Justice" she said loudly, holding up her right hand into a fist, as her Guests released their clasped hands, and held up their right hands in fists as well, "We are No longer just the United States of America, we are No longer just Canada, we are No longer Just Mexico, and we are No Longer Just the Sovereign Nation..!" she announced, pumping her fist in the air, then slapping the podium with her fist before grasping the wooden sides again, "We are the United Nation of Nations, and we will no longer live in fear, no longer live in inequality, and no longer be divided by walls or currency!" she said as she looked to her left, and saw her Guests stand firm with her, smiling and proud as the goosebumps over came their bodies, "and to those who try and stand in our way of this Unity, be warned, your time of hatred is done! Your time of oppression is over! Your time, ends, NOW!" she said, as the small crowd before her stood, applauding loudly, and smiling at the idea and thought of finally living in harmony without fear of retaliation, and finally a potential future they could believe in, and trust.

Looking to her left, and seeing the three Leaders standing and applauding her speech, Leticia smiled, took two steps back from the podium, and turned her attention to the audience, began to smile, and froze when she heard three pops in the distance, "Ugghh.." she heard to her left, turned her head quickly, and saw the three Leaders fall backward, hitting the floor of the podium with red beginning to form on their chest through their shirts. Dropping to her knees quick, and scrambling to their sides, she realized it was too late as she screamed, "Help! Where did that come from! WHITE!!! Where is Agent White!!???" she screamed as she put her hands on the Chief's chest, "Stay with me, stay with me.." she pleaded, her hands pooling with blood as she did her best to stop the bleeding of the Nations Leader.

Several hours later, while on the Helicopter back to the White House, Leticia's phone rang as the face of the device lit up in her lap. Looking down at the screen, she saw it was the Agent in White, took a deep breath, exhaled, slid the green icon to the right, and pressed the speaker icon, "Yeah..?" she said sadly.

"Morin and Colon are gone" the voice announced, and paused.

Leticia shook her head slowly, closed her eyes, and began rubbing her forehead, "And Chief Bear?" she asked, not able to stop thinking of the 'pops' she heard, and the noises the victims made as they were hit, and fell back.

"He was lucky, his heart was abnormal, and more in the middle of his chest" the voice said, and paused again for a moment, "but, he will be fine, and is in surgery now" the voice continued, and paused again.

Leticia shook her head and sighed, "Thank God" she said happily, removing her hand from her forehead, and looking at the screen as it went dark, "Stay with him, you hear me?" she said almost demanding, "and when he's out of surgery, bring me Roxie" she said, pressed the screen until it illuminated again, and pressed the red icon to hang up before the Agent could reply, "That bitch is mine" she said as she looked out the window, seeing the building of Washington D.C. pass by in the distance, and grateful she was almost home.

At midnight, Leticia's phone rang next to her large, comfortable bed, waking her. Rolling over and seeing the illuminated screen, she saw it was her Agent again, pressed the button to answer, and heard a female voice, "We are in your office, Madam President" Roxie's voice said, confusing the President as she lay there. Leticia pressed the red icon to hang up, pulled the thick blankets off her, flung her legs from the bed, slipped her feet into her house-slippers, rose from the bed, reached for her thick robe, donned it, and left her room to walk to her office.

Escorted by four Agents in Yellow with yellow ties, Leticia reached the Oval Office, opened the door, and saw Roxie on her knees, hands bound behind her back, with the Agent in White next to her, the Agent in Yellow with the Pink Tie, and the Agent in Red behind the Agent in White. The three stood there looking as professional and menacing as ever, which even gave Leticia goosebumps.

Walking passed Roxie, and not taking her gaze off the traitor, Leticia sat behind her desk, peered at the woman on her knees, and growled, "Why!?" she demanded, placing her hands on her desk.

Roxie looked scared, confused as to why she was there, "I, I have no idea wha.." she began and paused when she saw Leticia open the drawer to her desk, and remove the envelopes, tossing them across her desk so they slid and feel to the knees of Roxie, "Try again.." she said in a stern voice.

Roxie froze, her face looking dumbfounded as to how they knew, and then looked at the Agent in Yellow and Pink, "I, I'm so sorry Cousin" she wept, the tears falling quickly as she knew her days were numbered no matter what she said.

The Agent in Yellow and Pink removed the Fedora and face-visor quick, ripping off the Yellow head-covering, and glaring at the woman on her knees, "Don't you fucking dare call me your cousin!" she screamed as she stepped forward, pulled back her right arm, and threw the hardest punch she had ever thrown, connecting to the cheekbone of Roxie, and watching the bound woman fall to her side, "You make me sick you fucking coward!" she screamed, as the Agent in White reached out to stop Moxie from further assault.

Leticia watched for a moment, and smiled at the action she just witnessed, tapping her fingernails on the desk, looking at the Agent in Red, and nodding, "Pick her up, please" she asked, and watched as the Agent in Red obliged.

Roxie was lifted to her feet, and stood there, bleeding from her cheek as she whimpered from the assault, "I, I swear, I had no choice" she cried, her voice quaking as she mumbled, her head lowering in shame.

"You had every fucking choice!" Moxie screamed as she lunged forward to hit her relative again, and was stopped quick by the Agent in White.

"Easy Mox.." Leticia said casually as she looked at the furious Agent, then back to Roxie, "but she's right, Roxie, you had every choice, and could have come to us, right?" she asked, trying to persuade the scared and injured woman before her to calm down.

Roxie did her best to calm, but was having difficulty as she began hyperventilating, "I... I..." she stuttered, as her head began to sway, and she fainted to the floor without warning.

Leticia watched the scared Secretary fall, and nearly hit her head on the desk, as she looked at the Agent in White, "Get her home, put her in bed.." she said casually and calmly, "and put those back in her apartment where you found them.." she said as she nodded to the envelopes of cash on the floor near the collapsed body, "and please, do it as quietly as possible, we don't need any other problems at the moment" she said as she watched the three Agents pick up the Secretary, and carry her out of the Office, "Moxie? Please, stay.." she said, and watched as the Agents in White and Red took control of the limp woman, leaving Moxie to speak with their Boss.

Moxie stopped, turned, and went to stand before Leticia, "Yes, Ma'am?" she asked, standing rigid before the President, still fuming at the news she had just witnessed.

Leticia stood and watched the other three leave the Office, walked around her desk, and stand in front of Moxie, "We will find out what happened, okay?" she said softly, hoping to sooth the angered woman before her, "This, man, Larry, is not someone many can say no too, you understand?" she asked, hoping the question would help ease the mind of the woman in front of her.

Moxie looked towards the door and saw the feet of her cousin being drug from view, then looking at Leticia again, "I want Holly's job, Ma'am" she said, thinking about the ways she could relieve the anger and frustration she had building in her soul.

Leticia thought for a moment, and smiled, "We, already have an Agent in Red" she replied, and nodding slowly, "but, I think Holly would have approved.." she said as she patted Moxie on the shoulder and smiled, "but, you can't lose the Pink accents, understand?" she asked as she turned, and walked back to her chair, giving Moxie a chance to think about the request.

Moxie smiled slowly, looking at the Fedora on the floor where she had thrown it before the attack, "I wouldn't have it any other way, Ma'am" she said, raising her hand to her brow to salute her Boss, then lowering it sharply, and standing at ease.

Leticia smiled, and gave a gradual salute in return, "Good, because those two will be busy for a while, and we have some work to do here" she said, and offered Moxie the seat across from her with a gesture of her hand.

The Agents snuck Roxie into her apartment, tucked her in bed, put the envelopes back in their hidden spot, and left as quietly as they had entered. The next morning, the Agent in Red knocked on the door to the apartment, and waited. No answer. The Agent knocked again, and again, no answer. Checking the door knob, the Agent realized the door was unlocked as the door slowly pushed open, and stopped. The Agent in Red, slowly entered, walked through the apartment to the bedroom, and saw that Roxie was gone. Pulling a phone from their pocket, the Agent sent a message to the Agent in White that read; She's gone, the envelopes are gone, and there are no signs of a struggle.

Chapter 11

A bucket of ice-cold water was thrown on the face of the hooded figure sitting in a tall-backed chair, their arms outstretched and tied in several spots to long, thick boards. The torso was strapped to the chair, as the ankles were bound as well, nearly cutting off the circulation to the limbs. Another bucket of ice-cold water was thrown again, and this time, alerting the hooded figure awake.

"Wha..what.! Who is there?!" the female voice sounded as the voice trembled in fear.

"Roxie, Roxie, Roxie.." Larry said as the hood was removed, revealing the blonde as she sat in the chair nude, a bright light above her nearly blinding her from those in the room, "What did you tell Leticia?" he asked quickly, getting to the point.

Roxie shook her head, the water dripping down her face to her naked body, as her voice began to quiver, "Noth.. nothing.." she whimpered as she saw Larry standing before her.

Larry scoffed and smirked, "I find that really, really hard to believe.." he sighed as he stepped forward, and touched the cut on her cheek.

Roxie tried moving her head, and couldn't, "Wh... why would I lie?" she sighed, closing her eyes as she felt his fingers touch her face, and felt him press harder against her wound, "AAHHHHHH! FUCK!" she screamed, the tears beginning to fall down her face at the pain.

Larry pressed slightly harder, and quickly pulled his hand away, looking at the blood on his finger-tip, licking it, and chuckling, "Come on, Roxie" he said with a sinister tone in his voice that sent shivers down her spine, "Please, don't make me do something I know you will regret" he laughed, and looked to his right.

Roxie forced her eyes to look to her left, and saw a tall man, with blonde hair, glasses, wearing a black shirt and tan pants, standing in front of a table with his back to her, and she started to whimper even louder, "Fuck, Larry! Fuck! I didn't tell that bitch anything! I swear!" she screamed and pleaded, watching the man pick up a vial and a syringe, place it in the vial, and extract whatever was in it.

Larry watched the process, and smiled as he looked back at Roxie, "This, this is Gunther, the grandson of one of the SS Doctors" he introduced, and watched the man in the black shirt turn, and nod towards the prisoner, "who has come up with some really fun ways of making others talk" he said as he watched Gunther nod, turn back to the table, and reach for another vial.

Roxie wiggled in her chair like a rabbit trying to free itself from a trap, her tears cascading down her face as the fear set in deeper, "I swear, I swear, I swear" she pleaded as she tried to force herself free, the straps tightening as she did, pumping me with 'truth-serum' isn't going to help!" she announced and pleaded.

Larry laughed as he watched Gunther place the second vial down, and reach for a third, "Ha ha ha" he laughed and scoffed, "Truth-serum?" he chuckled and looked back at Roxie, "we, we haven't used that shit in, what? Decades? Right?" he asked the man at the table, and watched Gunther blindly nod over his shoulder.

Roxie stopped squirming for a moment, and thought about what was being drawn into the syringe, "Then, what?" she asked, not sure she wanted to know, the fear high in her voice as she watched Gunther set the third vial down, turn to face her, and lightly shake the syringe.

Larry smiled, "This one?" he asked, smirking as he chuckled and watched Gunther walk towards Roxie and reach for her arm, "This one has a little heroin.." he began nonchalantly, "a little PCP.. a little meth.." he said as Gunther gripped the back of Roxie's arm, and pressed the tip of the needle to her skin.

"Wait, wait, wait!" Roxie exclaimed as sshe felt the sharp point touch her arm, "I, I know things" she exclaimed, hoping it would stall the process.

Gunther paused for a moment and looked at Larry, "Sir?" he asked in a slight German-accent.

Larry nodded slightly, "Don't worry, I have the Narcan in my pocket" he reassured as he patted his pocket, "Proceed" he demanded, and watched as the sharp needle entered her arm, and the contents slowly injected in her blood stream.

Roxie watched it for a second, and then began to blink slowly as the effects were almost instantaneous. Her head began to jerk in the head-restraint, as her body began to convulse wildly for a few moments, her jaw clenching tightly as Larry heard several teeth break from the convulsions, and then, without warning, her body go limp as her eyes rolled back in her head.

"Four, three, two.." Larry counted backwards as he withdrew the Narcan spray bottle from his pocket, and place it towards her right nostril, "One.." he finished as he squeezed the bottle in her nostril, and stepped back, watching her eyelids spring open.

"Hwaaaaaaaa!" Roxie inhaled loudly as she sprang back to life instantly, and begin to convulse slightly in her chair, coughing loudly and uncontrollably, her eyes wide as she starred blankly at the man before her.

"Ahhh, there she is" Larry said gladly, a smile growing across his face as the prisoner came back to life, "Poor Roxie" he said soothingly as he took a step towards the naked woman strapped to the chair, "You have no idea what you got yourself into, do you?" he asked rhetorically, and chuckled, "A little Pawn, playing in the big world of Chess" he laughed as he reached out, and pressed his finger to the wound on her cheek again, "What did you tell Leticia?" he asked, pressing his finger into her flesh, and slightly under the skin, stretching the gash open.

"AAHHHHHHHHH!!!!" Roxie screamed in agony as she could feel the finger touching the cheekbone and pulling the skin away from her face, her fists clenching under the straps attached to her wrists, "FUUUCCKKKKK! AAHHHHHHHH! NOTHING!!!" she exclaimed loudly, trying to move her head and failing.

"You told somebody, something.." Larry replied as he slowly withdrew his finger from her face, looked at the bloody fingertip again, and wiped it on the chest of his shirt, "Moxie? What did you tell the whore cousin of yours?" he demanded as he looked at Gunther, "You have the second needle ready?" he asked, and waited.

Gunther held up a second syringe over his shoulder, flicked it lightly, and turned to face the menacing Boss, "Sir.." he said, and stepped forward again.

Roxie's eyes got wider, "Fuck.." she said in a groggy and deep tone, "I, I swear, no one knows anything" she pleaded, "How could they know anything I don't know?" she asked, watching Gunther walk towards her with the syringe, "You didn't tell me shit, so what could I tell them?" she asked and pleaded, the tears falling down her cheek again, hitting the would on her face, making her cry that much more.

Gunther reached Roxie's arm again, and looked at Larry, "Do you have the Narcan, Sir?" he asked Larry, and watched Larry pat his other front pocket.

"Right here" Larry smiled, "Continue, please" he asked, and watched as Gunther proceeded.

Roxie watched the needle press her skin again, just below the first injection spot, and tried to move her arm.

"If you move, and this needle breaks in your arm.." Gunther announced in his accent, and chuckled, "I will get another, and inject your insignificant chest flesh" he said, reaching out and flicking her erect left nipple.

Roxie froze at the flick, and starred at the evil man, "What, is that?" she asked as she watched the sharp point press into her flesh again.

Gunther smiled as the needle was pressed slowly into her arm, "This one?" he asked as he sounded pleased with himself at the act, "Morphine, Heroin, liquid-Psilocybin, and Polio.." he said as the liquid was slowly injected into her, withdrawing the needle, and stepping back.

"Polio?" Larry asked with a chuckle, "Nice touch" he added and laughed, "How do you come up with these things?" he asked, and watched Gunther smile, and return to the table as the mad-doctor tossed the syringe into a trash can under the table.

Gunther chuckled and patted an open book on the table, and reached for another syringe.

Roxie began convulsing immediately, as her pupils widened, and her mouth fell open, the drool beginning to pour from the corners of her mouth as her body went still.

"Wow.." Larry said as he witnessed her breathing quicken, then slow, and her eyelids blinked wildly, and her eyes rolled back slowly into her head again, "How long do you think it wil.." he began to asked, and stopped when he saw her chest stop moving, "Wow, Gunther, you are a genius" he said, and stepped forward, withdrawing the second Narcan from his front pocket.

"This is nothing, Sir" Gunther replied as he began to fill the third syringe from another set of vials, "this one, is my masterpiece" he cooed as he set down the first vial, and reached for the second.

Larry smiled and looked back at Roxie's limp and drooling body, her nipples erect as her body began to sweat. Placing the Narcan to her nostril again, Larry squeezed quickly, and stepped back once again. Moments later, Roxie came back to life with the same reaction she had the first time.

"HWWAAAAAAAAAA!" Roxie inhaled violently, and began jerking and squirming wildly and uncontrollably in her chair as her head began to rock and shake in the strapped restraint, "AAHHHHHHHHHHH!!!" she screamed as her body could feel the effects, and her pupils remained dilated.

"My poor, poor Roxie" Larry sighed as he stepped forward, and watched the dazed and doped up woman nod in and out, nearly incoherent to her surroundings, "I have to say, as much as I don't want too.." he said, reaching out with his other hand, and touching the opposite side of her face that hadn't been attacked, "I believe you" he reassured, brushing her soft cheek with the back of his hand, "But, I also cant trust you anymore" he said sadly, removing his hand, and leaning in to kiss her lightly on the lips, before standing back a few steps, and looking at Gunther, "Is that one ready?" he asked in a serious tone.

Gunther turned from his table, held up the third syringe, and smiled, "You have the third Narcan?" he asked, beginning to walk towards Roxie again.

Larry shook his head, "Wont be needed" he said boldly, and watched as the evil doctor walked to Roxie again.

Roxie's dazed eyes could not comprehend what was about to happen to her. Her eyes were glassed over, her mouth gapped open as the drool continued to drain from the corners of her mouth, and blood began to slowly drip from her nostrils, "Bu…bu…noooo" she stammered before her eyes closed slowly.

Gunther grabbed the back of her arm once more, pressed the sharp needle to her skin just below the last injection mark, and looked at Larry.

"Drop her from the plane when she's out" Larry said as he watched the needle enter her arm, as he turned and walked away before the contents were injected. He knew she would not survive the injection, and the body wouldn't be found for a few days, but he had other fish to filet, "and bring me her cousin, she has some answers I need" he said, leaving the dark room, the sounds of the naked woman behind him convulsing in her chair for a few seconds, and then, nothing.

Chapter 12

It had been two weeks since the announcement of the unification of the four Nations, and the assassinations. While Leticia could feel the future of the idea slipping between her fingers like sand, she knew she had to stand firm, and wait. She had visited the hospital that Chief Dancing Bear had been admitted too during those two weeks, waiting patiently for an hour in the morning to see if, and when, he was could to wake from his coma. And while he had not waken, the prognosis was strong that he would make a full recovery.

Walking through the sliding-glass doors one Saturday morning, past the Nurse's station, trailed by the Agent in White, Agent in Red, and four Agents in Yellow, Leticia approached the elevators, pressed the 'UP' button, and waited. Moments later, the doors opened, she and the Agents in White and Red, and two in Yellow followed, leaving the other two Agents in Yellow to stand guard of the elevators with instructions to check I.D.s of anyone coming up, as the doors closed, the Fourth-Floor button was pushed, and the metal box began rising.

As the doors opened a few moments later, Leticia froze and was stunned to see a beautiful woman standing, and waiting for her.

"President Gonzalez.." the woman said, her face stern. The woman was tall, with light-olive skin, soft-caring eyes that were dark-brown, a scar on her chin just below her mouth, and two long-thick braids that hung down beside her face over her chest nearly reaching her belt. She was very beautiful as she stood there, wearing a purple shirt with buttons, blue-jeans, and black boots laced up past her ankles with a ring of light fur around the ankle.

Leticia was taken back for a moment at her beauty, smiled and nodded, and held up her hand to stop the Agent in White as they stepped forward to address the woman, "Yes, do I know you?" she asked, stepping off the elevators, followed by the four Agents, as the two Agents in Yellow stopped and stood guard on each side of the elevator doors.

The pretty woman reached a hand out, "I am Little Feather" she said, a slight smile growing across her face, "they call me Natasha, and the Nurse's tell you have been here every day to check on my Uncle Grizzly" she said, still holding out her hand.

Leticia took a deep breath, and sighed, as she reached out quickly to shake the woman's hand, "So nice to meet you, Natasha" she said, as her smile grew wide as well, "Chief Dancing Bear is your Uncle, huh?" she asked as the two women shook hands, and released after a few moments, "he said he didn't have much family left, but that he had a Niece, and a few grandkids" she said as the two women stood there for a moment, and turned slowly to walk towards the hospital room, followed by the Agents in White and Red.

Natasha nodded and smiled as she walked next to the Powerful woman, "Yeah, he is all we have as well" she said as she walked, "I just wanted to say, thank you, for all you have done, and the daily visits to check on him" she added, nodding again, "It... it means a lot" she said as they got closer to the room at the end of the hall.

Leticia smiled as the continued the walk in silence, letting the appreciation sink in for a moment, as they reached the door, and saw two Nurses checking on their patient, "This idea wouldn't have been possible without him" the President said happily as she watched the Nurse's finish their tasks, and slowly leave the room.

Natasha and Leticia entered the room, leaving the Agents outside the door to stand guard. Each woman walked to either side of the bed, smiled at each other, and looked at the resting Leader of the Sovereign Nation.

"I remember the day I got this scar.." Natasha said as she reached up and touched her chin, and chuckled, "Uncle Grizz was teaching me to ride my first horse, and I fell forward hitting my chin on the saddle-horn" she chuckled as she smiled, "and he said, 'Every great A-Gichi Da needs a has a scar, to tell a story'.." she said as she tried to imitate his deep voice and accent.

Leticia smiled at the story, and asked, "A-Gichi Da?" she asked as she looked up at Natasha.

Natasha smiled, "It means, 'Female Warrior'.." she said proudly, standing taller as she accepted her title.

Leticia smiled at the translation, and could feel herself become prouder at the idea the man laying before her had handed down such great beliefs to a strong woman, "He sounds like he was a Warrior himself" she said, as she turned her attention back to the Chief as he lay unconscious.

Natasha smiled as she removed her hand from her chin, and smiled, "There are stories" she laughed.

A moment later, Chief Dancing Bear's head moved and shifted slightly, a slight and light moan grumbling from his throat as he licked his lips gently, and his eyelids began to gently move and twitch.

The women stood there in shock for a moment, as they watched, and waited patiently, almost too nervous to say anything, as the Chief slowly began to come to life.

"Uncle?" Natasha said softly, not wanting to scare the Leader as he slowly came too.

The Chief slowly batted his eyes as they opened, peacefully and confusingly starring at the ceiling for a few moments, licking his lips, and looking to his left to see Natasha standing there, "Nishimis..?" he asked slowly in a groggy voice as his vision became cleared, and he could see the beautiful woman standing before him, "Little Feather.." he said slowly as a slight and weak smile crept across his face.

Natasha smiled big, as a few tears of joy ran down the woman's face, "Inzhishenh.." she cooked as she placed her hand on his, though it covered with tape to hold down the wires and tubes protruding from the top of his hand, "I am here" she said softly, leaning in to kiss the old man on his cheek, and stand back up, still holding his hand gently.

Leticia watched the interaction for a moment, and thought about leaving to let the two family members reunite after the tragedy.

Chief Dancing bear slowly looked to his right, and saw Leticia standing there and about to turn and leave, "Boozo Neeji" he said softly, blinking a few times, and slightly nodding his head in the gentlest of ways, "You, are here too..?" he asked, smiling a little more.

Natasha smiled, and turned her attention to Leticia for a moment, "She, has been here everyday to check on you" she said soothingly, and looked back at her Uncle, "She cares" she added, her smile not fading as the tears slowly fell from her eyes, down her chin, and hitting the blanket on the bed that covered the Great Chief.

Chief Dancing Bear blinked a few times, and nodded as he closed his eyes, "Chi Migwech.." he said slowly, opening his eyes, leaning his head back, "Can, can I have some water?" he asked, licking his lips as his voice sounded raspy.

Leticia took a few steps towards the side-table, poured some water from the pitcher into the small, plastic cup, and handed it to Natasha with a smile, "I, I think this should be your honor" she said, reaching the cup out.

Natasha smiled, released her Uncle's hand, took the cup, and placed it to his lips softly, gently tipping the cup to allow the water to slowly reach his lips, and let him drink at his speed, "Little bit at a time, okay?" she cooed with a smile, tipping the cup back after a few seconds to allow the Chief to swallow and relax.

Leticia smiled at the interaction, and nodded, "I will be back tomorrow, okay?" she asked, placing her hand on the blanket next to the Chief's hand closest to her.

Chief Dancing Bear nodded slowly, and blinked a few times, then looked at Leticia, "Did, did they catch the shooter?" he asked, his voice still weak and raspy.

Leticia nodded slowly, "We, did.." she replied softly with a hint of a smile, "and we wanted to make sure you were awake before we proceeded with the execution" she added as she gently touched his hand, not wanting to cross any boundaries.

Natasha watched the slow and gentle embrace, and smiled as she set the cup down on the table next to her.

Chief Dancing Bear turned his attention to the ceiling again, and closed his eyes, "Good.." he whispered, and paused, the slowly opened his eyes again, turning his attention to Leticia, "I, I would like Little Feather to take my place, until.." he stammered and paused, closing his eyes for a moment, and looking at her again, "until, I can regain my place at your side.." he said, turning his hand slowly to allow the Presidents hand to lay in his palm.

Leticia smiled and looked at Natasha, "It would be an Honor" she replied with a nod, and looked back at the

Chief as he lay there, his face and body tired, "An Honor" she repeated with a slight nod, and a brighter smile.

Chief Dancing Bear closed his eyes at the answer, the smile creeping across his face wider for a moment, then opening his eyes, and starring directly into the soul of Leticia, "And, please.." he ushered as he held her hand firmly in his, "I, want her to be that man's executioner.." he said firmly, his smile fading as he became more serious for a moment.

Leticia looked at Natasha, who's eyes were swollen and red from the tears, as the A-Gichi Da stood taller, ready to accept her task, "As you ask" the President replied, nodding to Natasha, then back to the Great Chief, and gently squeezed his hand to confirm the request.

The Great Chief smiled, leaned his head back, and closed his eyes, "It is done" he said, and slowly drifted back to sleep.

The two women stood there and watched the Great Man slowly drift back to sleep, his chest and stomach slowly rising and falling, as the deep breathing and light snore filled the room.

A week later, as Leticia was sitting in the Oval Office, her phone rang which startled her, as she looked at it for two-rings, cocked her head with confusion, reached for the receiver, picked it up, and placed it to her ear, "Hello?" she asked as her face contorted with confusion.

"So, he survived.." Larry said with a chuckle, "Cant say the same for Roxie, though can you?" he asked with a chuckle, "Cant save them all, Leticia" he added, as the phone clicked on the other end, and the dial tone sounded in her ear.

Leticia hung up the phone, her brow furrowed from frustration, as she pressed the intercom button, "Anita!?" she asked in a demanding tone.

"Ma'am?" the confused voice on the other end replied.

"Come in here" Leticia added, and released the button.

A moment later, the door to the Oval Office opened, and entered the new Secretary, a short, brunette woman with large hips, wearing a floor length green dress, wearing glasses the sat on the tip of her nose, "Ma'am?" she asked as she entered holding a clipboard and pen.

"Why didn't you warn me of the call?" Leticia asked, sounding frustrated as she glared at the new Secretary.

"Ma'am?" Anita asked, looking confused.

Leticia looked at the phone and pointed to it, then quickly turning her attention to Anita while still pointing at the phone, "This phone, rang" she said frustratingly.

Anita looked at the phone, then at her Boss, "Ma'am, I didn't forward any call" she added, clutching the clipboard to her small chest.

Leticia looked at Anita more confused, then at the phone, then back to Anita, "You, didn't?" she asked, sounding even more frustrated and confused.

"No, Ma'am" Anita replied calmly, clutching the clipboard tighter to her body.

Leticia shook her head, "Get me the Agent in White, please" she asked, shaking her head, and watched as Anita turned quickly to leave the Office, closing the door behind her.

Two days later, the intercom sounded in the Oval Office, as Leticia pressed the button, "Yes, Anita?" she asked, her voice calm.

"Ma'am, you have several guests here to see you.." the Secretary replied.

"Guests?" Leticia asked, sounding concerned and alert, "Do they have an appointment?" she asked, looking at the itinerary and shaking her head, "I, I don't have any meetings on my agenda.." she added and released the intercom button.

"Yes, Ma'am, but, these women insisted on seeing you" Anita added, and released the button.

Leticia looked confused for a moment, and pressed the button again, "Women?" she asked, "Umm, okay, show them in" she said and released the button, reaching for her coffee mug, and holding it in front of her.

A moment later, the door to the Oval Office, as Anita stood there in a blue dress that stopped at her knees, her hair in a bun, and the glasses resting at the tip of her nose, "Ma'am?" she asked as she stepped to the side, and watched as Natasha entered the Office, followed by two more women, "Ms. Feather, Mrs. Rachel Morin, and Mrs. Juanita Colon, here to see you.." she introduced as the three women entered the Oval Office, and once inside, Anita excused herself with a nod and a smile, closing the door behind her.

Leticia looked surprised, as she set her mug down, and stood, smiling at Natasha, "Boozo Neeji" she greeted with a nod, walking from her chair with her hand out reached to shake her new friend.

Natasha smiled as she reached her hand out as well, "Boozo Neeji!" she announced as the two women shook hands, and embraced for a short hug, "I, we, are sorry to intrude.." she said as the embrace ended, looking at the two women behind her, then back at the President, "but, this is important" she added, taking a step to the side.

Leticia gently shook her head, "Not at all, please, sit" she offered with a wave of her hand towards the chairs and sofa in the Office, "How is your Uncle?" she asked happily.

Natasha smiled and sat, "He is doing really well, thank you" she said, "and sends his blessings and light" she added as she crossed her right leg over her left knee, placing her folded hands on her top knee, "but we, aren't here for that" she added, her face becoming more serious.

Leticia smiled, and looked at the other two women, then back to Natasha, "What, can I do for you?" she asked, smiling and looking confused.

Juanita Colon was a short woman, with jet-black hair that was pulled back in a swirled bun, light-skin, dark-brown eyes, thick legs that wouldn't allow her to cross them, and wearing a simple gold necklace, and her wedding ring, with a gentle smile on her face. Her orange dress was ankle-length, with matching flat dress shoes on her feet.

Rachel Morin was a short woman, with short blonde-hair that was feathered on the sides like a 'Pixie-cut', freckles and dimples, wearing a red-dress that stopped below her knees, and she too had thick thighs that didn't allow her to cross her legs, but crossed her ankles as she sat to the side, with matching red pumps that added nearly two-inches to her short frame. Though her smile had yet to appear on her face.

"We.." Natasha began, and paused, looking at the women she arrived with.

"Ahem" Rachel Morin sounded as she cleared her throat to interrupt, "We, are here to pick up where our husbands left off" she said proudly, nodding to her two counterparts, and looking at Leticia, and finally smiling, "and, we have some ideas" she said, leaning forward slightly to show she meant business.

Leticia smiled, and scooted her rear back in her chair, "What do you have in mind?" she asked, crossing her left arm across her chest as her hand went under her armpit, her right elbow pressing against the back of her left hand, as she placed her right hand to her mouth in a relaxed fist, ready to listen to the women before her.

Chapter 13

With less than six-months until the end of Leticia's second Presidential term, the passing of Chief Dancing Bear from a massive heart attack, and the signing of the United Nation of Nations, the new Super Country sat and waited on pins and needles to see how the incorporation of Health Care, Enforced Laws and Rules, and Governments would cohabitate and integrate for the welfare of its citizens. The four Leaders, Leticia Gonzalez, Rachel Morin, Natasha Little Feather, and Juanita Colon, had the support and encouragement of the People, but not of the Upper Governments of their respective Governments and most of its Officials.

The Supreme Court of the US, had gone above and beyond to veto the signing of the UNN, as well as the House of Representatives, and Congress. Parliament of

Canada and its Government had followed suit in its rejections and refusals, as well as the Cartels threatening the Government of Mexico into denying the unifications. It seemed that only the Sovereign Native Nation had supported the pact, and would voice this at every chance they could.

That July 4th, four months before the Elections, the People would finally get their wish, as the four Women met in Washington D.C., at an undisclosed location, and would settle the dispute once and for all.

"How do we disband these Agencies?" Mrs. Colon asked, her accent thick as she sat on one side of an oval table, wearing a light brown dress, a pearl necklace with her deceased-husband's likeness dangling from a small medallion, and her hair styled in a traditional Mexican fashion.

Rachel Morin shook her head, and laughed, "We could fire them" she said seriously, sitting there opposite Juanita, wearing a purple dress with lavender polka-dots, and her hair pulled back in a ponytail, as she tapped her pen on the table.

Natasha laughed at the idea, "Is that even possible?" she asked, looking around the table, as she sat wearing and orange dress, with her traditional Native wrap of beautiful colors and designs, her hair in the braids she wore that hung down her face to her chest disappearing beneath the tabletop.

Leticia listened for a moment, shook her head at the discussion and ideas, and laughed, "These corrupt Agencies have obviously been bribed, and paid off" she interjected, interlocking her fingers in front of her as she rested her forearms on the edge of the oval table before her, "and, why not fire them?" she asked, looking at the faces of her counterparts, "If they have done nothing but fuck over the People from the beginning, why don't we make those decisions, as a Panel?" she asked, looking at the other three for opinions.

The three Women pondered the question as they looked at each other, the question swirling in their heads as the idea showed on their faces.

"Wouldn't we need a fifth?" Rachel asked, "In case there's a tie in votes?" she asked, looking around the table, "I mean, we may agree on a lot of things, right?"

she asked, making a point none had thought about, "but we wont always agree on everything" she added with a chuckle as she leaned back in her chair.

Natasha laughed as her body slightly bounced in her chair, "We, could flip a coin like they do in those football games before they start?" she joked, looking at Leticia who's Country had started the game and tradition.

The four Women laughed and shook their heads.

"Well, that's actually not a bad idea" Leticia laughed as she sat there, wearing a green dress, her hair covered in a purple head-wrap, and some diamond earrings showing, "I mean, why not, right?" she offered, "But, can we all agree to this? Knowing its not always going to go in our favor, but it is what is best for the People?" she asked, looking at the others.

Natasha, Rachel and Juanita looked at each other and thought for a few moments, and began nodding in agreement.

"Settled" Leticia laughed as she made a note on the paper before her.

"We all cant be the Head, right?" Juanita asked, blurting out the question to stop the laughs, and making a more serious inquiry, "We need a Person, or Woman, in charge, don't we?" she asked, looking at the others as they began thinking.

The table was quiet for a moment.

Leticia thought for a moment about a book she had read about Tyranny, and a chapter about 'Beware the One Party State', as she cleared her throat gently, set her pen down, and leaned forward slightly, "How long is this term for the new Leaders? Four Years? Eight?" she asked, looking around the table, "If we were each to take a year as the 'Head of Nation'.." she suggested, slightly shrugging her shoulders at the suggestion, and motioning with her hands, "giving the Head a new title of, say, Chancellor..?" she asked, looking around again to let the idea swirl in the pondering minds, and waiting for any rejections.

"Chancellor?" Rachel asked quickly, looking at the others, "Didn't, Germany try that once?" she asked, chuckling, "and how did that turn out?" she asked rhetorically, as her chuckle stopped, "and what, the others become, what, Vice Chancellors?" she suggested as she chuckled again.

Leticia nodded quickly, "Exactly" she replied, her voice serious, as she watched Rachel stop chuckling, "If we don't use the past as our example, then we are doomed to repeat it, right?" she asked, the question a valid one that seemed to resonate and make sense, "I get that 'absolute power corrupts absolutely', but.." she paused to wait for any feedback.

Natasha nodded, "I agree" she added, nodding to Leticia with a little smile, "There are ways we can make and fix laws, and with a title other than President, no offense.." she nodded with a laugh.

Leticia laughed and shook her head, "No offense taken, I didn't create the term" she added.

Juanita shook her head, "I, I don't know" she quipped, "I tend to agree with Rachel" she said as she looked at the woman across from her, "I don't want to be compared to a regime that was responsible for a few hundred thousand deaths" she began, and looked at Leticia.

Leticia dropped her pen at the statement, "A few, hundred thousand?" she asked, looking at the others, then at Juanita again, "Try, more than six-million!" she said with a hint of sorrow and excitement.

Juanita's jaw dropped as he stared at Leticia, then at the others, "Really? Six... million?" she asked startled.

"Yeah.." Natasha answered, shaking her head.

Juanita shook her head furiously, "Then no, no, sorry, I don't want to be associated with that" she added, being firm in her decision.

Leticia looked at the Agent in White by the door, "You, have a quarter?" she asked with a laugh, and watched as the Agent reached into their pocket and walked towards the table, withdrawing a coin, placing it on the table, and returning to the door to stand guard. Leticia picked up the coin, "This has two sides, right?" she asked, showing the coin to the others, "and it seems we have our first tie-breaker" she laughed as she looked at Juanita and Rachel, "One of you call it in the air, 'Heads', we go for it, 'Tails', we choose a different title, agreed?" she asked, looking at the three.

Natasha, Juanita, and Rachel all agreed, as Juanita nodded to Rachel, "You call it" she said, and leaned back to wait in anticipation.

Leticia positioned the coin on her thumb, and nodded to Rachel, "Ready?" she asked.

"As I'll ever be" Rachel laughed, as she watched Leticia flip the coin in the air, "Tails" she announced a second after Leticia flipped the coin.

The coin flipped in the air, over and over quickly, falling to the wooden table, making clinks and clonks, as it bounced several times, the sound of the metal coin tinking and slightly spinning in a flat-circle as it slowed, the icon slowly appearing as it gradually stopped.

"Heads" Natasha announced as the coin stopped, and the four Women looked at each other in agreement, nodded, and looked at Leticia who jotted the decision on her notepad.

"Now, how do we fire those fuckers in Government?" Leticia asked with a laugh as she looked at the faces of the next group of Powerful World Leaders.

Several days later, as Leticia was sitting in her office, starring out her window, the intercom on her Presidential-phone buzzed, looking at it with a puzzled look, and slowly reached for the receiver, picking it up, placing it to the side of her head, "Hello?" she asked slowly.

"They are leaving now, Ma'am" the male voice replied, not wasting any time.

Leticia shook her head, placing her free hand on her brow, and rubbing her brow and temple lightly, "I thought they weren't meeting until next week?" she replied out of confusion and frustration.

The phone was silent on the other end for a moment, "It's SCOTUS Ma'am, I don't think they had a choice" the voice replied, and was quiet again.

Leticia lowered her hand from her brow, spun slowly in her chair to look out the window and the sunny-day that was brightening the lawn, "Are, all Nine of them there?" she asked, watching several Agents patrol the grounds as a Landscaper rode a lawnmower in the distance.

"No Ma'am" the male voice replied quickly, "Judge Ashleene was not there" he said, and paused, "Should I bring her to you?" he asked, and waited again.

Leticia spun in her chair back to her desk, and looked at the planner in front of her, flipping a few pages ahead, then back to that date, "How many cars are those Eight in?" she asked, picking up a pen and jotting a note.

"Three" the male voice replied.

Leticia chuckled and smiled, "They don't make it back to the airport, understood?" she asked without a hint of questioning.

"Yes, Ma'am" the male voice replied.

Leticia shook her head as she finished writing, set her pen down, and looked at what she had just wrote, "And yes, please, bring me the Judge, and Holly's revolver, tomorrow" she said, and paused.

The phone was quiet for a moment, "Yes, Ma'am" the male voice replied, and the sound of the phone hanging up on the other end was the last thing Leticia heard.

The next day, Leticia was escorted from her Oval Office to the front of the White House by the Agent in White and the Agent in Red, where awaited a convoy of dark-vehicles, all bullet-proof with dark-windows. The rear-passenger door of the third vehicle was opened by an Agent in Yellow, as Leticia hopped into the vehicle, the door shut, and the escorting Agents got in the front seat, with the Agent in White driving.

"Is she here?" Leticia asked as she looked to the front two-seats.

The Agent in Red nodded, and pointed to the dark vehicle in front of them.

Leticia nodded, sat back, pulled her seatbelt across her chest, and clipped it into the safety latched on her hip, "And, Holly's gun?" she asked, looking out her window as the vehicle pulled away to follow the two in front of them.

The Agent in Red held up a small, Red, safety box with a combination lock, then lowered it again.

Leticia smiled, closed her eyes for a moment, and thought about her deceased friend.

After an hour of driving South, the convoy of vehicles turned down a long dirt-driveway, lined with cherry-trees, and lavender plants. Making several long and swooping turns along the long dirt-driveway, a small home appeared in the distance, with a large Weeping Willow tree in the yard not far from the home. The home was blue, with white trim, and a bright-red door, with a wrap-around porch, and several chairs decorating the wooden-covered porch. Under the tree, several sets of legs could be seen in the distance, and Leticia's heart began to race.

Pulling up to the home, the convoy of vehicles stopped, the Agents disembarked the vehicles all at the same time as if orchestrated to a rhythm, with the Agent in Red opening Leticia's door, and waiting for the President to unbuckle her seatbelt, and gracefully get out, with her green-flats hitting the ground at the same time. The Agent in Red handed Leticia the Red-lockbox, closed the door as Leticia took a few steps from the vehicle, and began walking towards the willow tree and its hanging limbs.

Standing under the tree, with her hands secured behind her back by a zip-tie, her black dress reaching her ankles as she stood there barefoot, her eyes red and scared as the most Powerful woman approached her.

"Why didn't you go with the others to their secret meeting with Larry?" Leticia asked as she took a few more steps across the lawn, stopping a few yards from the bound Judge.

Judge Rachel Ashleene was a 'Conservative-Liberal' from Iowa, who had grown up thinking both sides had the right ideas, and while she wanted reform and to bring back many of the 'Respectful Ideas' of the past, knew that growth for the future was important. Her bright-red hair and pale skin was a typical Iowa trait, but her thinking was very progressive.

"I... I, don't agree with Larry, or those others" Judge Ashleene replied, her voice quivering as she began to sweat, the tears slowly forming in the corners of her eyes at the unknown before her.

Leticia gently nodded at the remark, and looked at the Agent in White, who took a few steps forward, and slowly put their palms out. Leticia placed the Red-lockbox on the Agents palms, "Because, you are from Iowa?" she asked, spinning the combination lock, and pressing the latch to the side, hearing the lock click open.

Judge Ashleene watched the actions before her, as the menacing Agents stood around her, "Becau… because, I have a heart" she replied, her voice nervous as she stood in the middle, the low-hanging limbs just above her head.

Leticia nodded slowly, "A, heart, huh?" she asked, almost questioning the remark.

"Yes, yes Ma'am" the bound Judge replied, her voice shaking as the sweat began to sleep through the armpits of her dress, darkening the fabric.

As the lid to the Red-lockbox was lifted, Leticia smiled at the comment, "I, too, have a heart.." she began as the large, fifty-caliber handgun appeared, "and I was a little confused as too why you wouldn't go to the meeting, and listen to the hatred and ramblings of the man who wanted to destroy the world, for greed.." she said, lifting the large handgun from the box, and examining it in her left hand, "power... money.." she said, as she looked at the bound Judge, "then, I looked at your financials, bank holding, property listings.." she said, looking at the gun again, "and thought, 'Why?'.." she said, turning her attention to the Judge again, then to the Agent in Yellow behind her, and nodded.

The Agent in Yellow pulled a small pair of snips from a jacket-pocket, took a few steps towards the bound Judge, reached out, and cut the plastic restraints from her wrists. The zip-tie fell to the ground as the Agent in Yellow placed the snips back in their pocket, and took a few steps back to their spot, unbuttoned their jacket in the front, and swung the jacket open revealing a holstered Desert Eagle gun to let the Judge know she was being watched, and guarded.

Leticia smiled and nodded a 'Thank you' to the Agent in Yellow, and looked at the Judge, her eyes intently starring into the soul of the woman before her, "There, is this game.." she said as she reached into the red-box still held by the Agent in White, and withdrew a large round of ammunition, "I am sure you have heard of it.." she said as she flung the gun to the side, and watched the revolver chamber pop-out, sliding the round into one of the six-empty holes, "Russian Roulette.." she said as she reached into the box again, and withdrew an empty casing, "Where, as we know.." she said as she slid the empty shell into the space next to the 'live' round, and reached for another empty casing, "Is more a game of, luck.." she said with a smile, and reached for a third empty casing, sliding it next to the second, then another, and finally, a fifth and last.

The Judge watched the President finish filling the voids in the revolver, and snap her wrist to close the gun with a 'CLICK', and spin the revolvers round chamber, her eyes watering as the sweat continued to soak her dress, outlining her under-boob and stomach, "Wha... what do you want?" Judge Ashleene pleaded as she watched the Agent in White close the red-lockbox, and hand it to the Agent in Red, take the large handgun from the President, and approach the Judge.

Leticia stood motionless for a moment, her smile widening across her face as she watched her favorite Agent approach the scared Judge, "I want to know if I can trust you" she said sternly as the Agent in White stood next to the scared Judge, "I want to know, how much, 'for the people', you are.." she said as she watched the Agent in White hold out their hand to offer the gun to the Judge.

Judge Ashleene looked at the President, then at the gun, then up to the face-visor of the Agent in White, then back to the President, "An...and, how is this supposed to prove that?" she asked, her voice trembling in fear as to what was about to be asked of her.

Leticia smirked and nodded slowly, "Take it, place it to your temple..." she said softly, as if she was trying to soothingly coerce the Judge, "And pull the trigger.." she said casually, as if the action was nothing to be worried about.

The Judge looked at the President for a moment as if the woman in power was joking, then at the gun, and paused, "And, if I refuse?" she asked, looking back at the President.

Leticia nodded, and without a word, every Agent in Yellow surrounding the two women, pulled their large handguns, and pointed them at the Judge, "Your choice.."

she said, smiling as she took a step back to be clear of any Agent behind her.

Judge Ashleene gasped, and held her breath for a moment at the comment and actions around her, looked at the Agent in White with fear on her face and in her eyes, and slowly reached out for the large gun. Feeling the weight of the metal object, she nearly dropped it as her arm fell to her side. Looking at the President again, hoping the woman in power would change her mind, the Judge pleaded once more, "Please, you.. they, don't have to do this.." she said, her voice quavering as it cracked from the stress and fear that poured from her body and eyes.

Leticia held up her right-hand, and without a word, the hammers of the surrounding guns cocked, as the Agent's readied their stances and aimed at the Judge.

The Judge whimpered loudly as she slowly raised the gun to her temple, and paused, closing her eyes as the cold-metal touched the side of her head.

"Pull it once.." Leticia said softly, as if the action was nothing to be afraid of, "and if, 'IF', you live.." she said, her voice reassuring and sweet, "I will know, you, love the people that you are, well, were, sworn to protect.." she said with a slight smile growing under her nose.

Judge Ashleene trembled at the words as they entered her ears, the tears falling down her face as the sweat continued to pour from her pores, and her bladder emptied down her legs to fill her shoes, and to the grass below her. Her hand shook, as she mumbled a soft prayer, clenched her eyes tighter, and pulled the trigger.

'CLICK!' sounded the trigger as the hammer slammed against an empty round.

The Judge dropped the gun to the ground out of fear, and fell to her knees, sobbing as her knees hit the urine-soaked grass below her, "Fuuuuuuucckkkk, no!" she screamed as she covered her face with her hands, sobbing uncontrollably, as she heard the guns around her being holstered.

Leticia watched the scared Judge fall to her knees, crying, and mumbling as she prayed, "What did Larry want with the other Judges?" she asked, and waited for a few moments, shifting her weight and taking a step forward.

Judge Ashleene sobbed for another moment, sniffled, and looked up at the President, tears falling from the scared woman's face, as snot dripped from her nose to her upper lip, her eyes red and her face scared, "He.." she began and paused, looking at the Agent in White's boots next to her, then back to the President, "he wanted them, us, to overthrow you" she stammered, looking at the boots next to her, and didn't move, scared of the person next to her.

Leticia shook her head at the idea of a Coup, and scoffed, "And you.." she said, shaking her head, "didn't want too?" she asked in disbelief, watching the face of the Judge on her knees to see her reaction to the question.

Judge Ashleene wiped her eyes, and drug her arm across her face to wipe her nose and lip of the snot that had been running down, looked up at Leticia with nervous and scared eyes, "Ask.." her voice trembled, "ask the other Justices, and they will tell you.." she stammered, hoping her words would convince the President.

Leticia shook her head and chuckled slightly, "That, isn't even an option at this point" she replied, watching the confusion on the Judge's face before her, "you, are all that's left" she stated, and watched as Judge Ashleene's face went to shock and amazement.

"What, do you mean, I am all that's left?" the Judged asked surprised and curiously, raising her torso up a little, as her rear came away from her heels.

Leticia took a few steps forward, and reached out her hand to offer the Judge help up from her knelt position of fear, "There, was an accident" she said, smiling softly, her arm and hand still extended, "And, as I said.." she stated, gently shaking her opened hand for the Judge to take, "You, are all that's left", she finished.

Judge Ashleene looked at the President in her eyes, and could feel the truth coming from her voice, as she looked at the extended hand, and slowly reached out, taking the hand, and being pulled up from her knees. Wiping her face once more, blinking a few times, and looking around at the Agents surrounding them, Judge Ashleene shook her head, closed her eyes for a moment to ponder what was next, opened them, and did her best to compose herself, "What, what do I do now?" she asked, releasing the hand that helped her up.

Leticia smiled and nodded, "Now, we get to work, and relieve Larry of what he holds most dear and precious" she said as she tilted her head slightly, and nodded as she turned to walk back to the convoy of vehicles.

Judge Ashleene's face looked puzzled and confused for a moment as she watched the President turn and begin to walk away, "What.. what would that be?" she asked, beginning to take a few steps to follow her Boss.

Leticia continued to walk forward, nearing the vehicle she arrived in, paused for a second, turned her head over her left shoulder, and smiled a devious grin, "Power" she said as she opened the door for herself, mounted into the vehicle, and shut the door with authority.

Chapter 14

The sun was barely peeking through the clouds on that mid-October morning, with less than two weeks until Halloween, and a little over three weeks until the Election for the new Presidency, Leticia sat in the Oval Office, wearing a light purple knee-length dress, White flats, and her hair pulled back into a tight bun, starring out the window, and waiting for her guests to land for their last meeting before the Election.

Leticia had high hopes for the Country, and its future, though she would not be the one in charge after the next election. The ideas and procedures she, and the wives of the assassinated leaders of the three Nations that were joining America to create The Nation of Nations, would make the new Country stronger than any populated Country since the Roman Empire. The name, 'Nation of Nations' would later be changed to something that would fit the common and overall goal.

Leticia had always loved to arrive at her office before the Secretary was at her desk, mainly to have some quiet and enjoy the morning before the hectic day began, but also, to go over the day before, and prepare herself for the busy burdens of the schedule at hand. She had sent her favorite Agent, the Agent in White, to be a guest at the Military graduations of the Five Branches of Service, Army, Navy, Coast Guard, Air Force, and Marines, and since the Agent's oldest son was graduating from the Marines Boot Camp, she felt it fitting that the Agent be there to support that child, even though the child thought the Agent was dead.

'Riiiiiinnngggg', came the sound of the phone on the desk of the President, confusing her for a moment. 'Riiiiinnnnggggg', sounded the phone again, as Leticia looked at the noisy square-object, and tilted her head, slowly reaching for it. She had never been called that early in the morning before, and since Anita, the Secretary, was not at her desk, she was quite skeptical about answering it.

"Good morning" Leticia answered sweetly as she placed the receiver to her ear, and reached for her morning cup of coffee she had made herself.

"Mmhghmmmm" the sound came from the other end, as if someone was clearing their throat, "You, think there wouldn't be consequences" the male voice answered.

Leticia stopped reaching for her cup for a moment, and looked at the phone intently, "Larry?" she asked, looking at the caller-id and seeing it was a local number, "How.." she began and paused.

"You take my Justice's away, abruptly, and quite maniacally, if I may say" Larry chuckled and paused, "You have balls, Madam President" he said and paused again.

Leticia heard a sound in the distance, and spun slowly to look out the window again, seeing the helicopter with her guests approaching, "Like, something you haven't done before?" she asked, turning to reach for her coffee again, picking up the cup, and placing it to her lips, "I mean, come on.." she added after a sip, and placing the cup down on the coaster it came from, "Look what you did to Roxie, you sick fuck" she snarled with a chuckle, remembering the traitor that once served her.

There was a slight chuckle on the other end, "Roxie, she was a pawn, a twig that was easily broken by dangling some shiny objects in front of her, like a hungry fish ready to be fileted.." Larry snarked, and the sound of sipping could be heard through the phone.

Leticia's brow furrowed for a moment, as she listened to the helicopter get closer, and stop high-above the White House lawn.

"You take my Justice's away.." Larry began again quickly, "and try to turn my last remaining one against me with the promise of 'Power'..?" he quipped with a chuckle, "What kind of fucking power do you think you really have?" he asked as he paused, the sound of him sipping again could he be heard, a little louder this time.

Leticia listened to the man on the other end of the phone, and to the helicopter's blades swirling loudly outside the White House, "I have as much Po.." she began.

"You have shit, Leticia" Larry interrupted quickly, "but, your guests are here.." he said and paused for a moment, "Enjoy your meeting" he said with a chuckle, and the line went silent with the click of the phone hanging up.

Leticia's face contorted with confusion, as she reached out to hang up the phone slowly, pushed her large chair with wheels back slowly, spun, and stood to look out the window to the helicopter hovering almost one-hundred feet off the ground. The side-metal door opened, and without warning, the three wives of the assassinated leaders, Little Feather, Rachel Morin, and Juanita Colon, a long with Judge Ashleene, were all pushed from the door, falling to the ground beneath them, and hitting the grass with a loud and explosive 'THUD', before the door was shut, and the helicopter flew away into the brisk October morning.

That same morning, on the other side of the country in San Diego, California, the Agent in White stood on the parade ground of the United States Marine Corps Recruit Depot, and watched the several Platoons do their morning exercises, practice marches, and disappear into the barracks behind the bleachers, as the families and friends stood behind the thick, metal chains as they took zoomed-in pictures of their Recruit. As the Recruits disappeared into their barracks, the Agent in White led the families to the bleachers, along with other Marine Drill Instructors and Staff, and waited for the ceremony to begin.

Standing in front of the Parade Review Box, surrounded by the Officers and Dignitaries, the Agent in White stood front and center, and watched as the Recruits became Marines during their Pass and Review, saluting each Platoon as it marched by, watching those deemed "The Few, and Proud" return the salute to the Review Box, and Agent.

The Platoons stopped on their marks in unison, performed a 'Right Face', and stood at attention, facing the crowd of families and friends, with the stern look of Pride chiseled on their faces. As the Major of the Base stepped to the microphone to introduce the Platoons, he paused for a brief moment, and watched as the Agent in White moved from their spot, and slowly marched towards the first row of the Platoon in front where the

Agent stood. Reaching the end of the Platoon, the Agent made a sharp 'Left-Face', and marched slowly down the line, and stopped in front of one of the New Marines, performed a sharp 'Right-Face', and faced the Marine, standing less than two-feet from the young man in his sharp new uniform of a Tan Shirt, Blue Pants, Black Shoes, and sharp White Cover with the Marine Emblem shiny in the front. Raising the right hand to the brim of the White Fedora, the Agent gave a sharp salute to the new Marine, and paused.

The new Marine watched nervously for a moment, unsure of why he was receiving the honor, and without question, returned the salute as sharp as he was given one, as his face turned red, his eyes swollen for a moment, and the two dropped their salutes in unison.

As the Agent approached, so did the Agent leave, with a 'Right-Face', a slow and steady march down the row to the end, another sharp 'Right-Face', and back to the spot where the Agent stood moments before, paused, performed a sharp 'About-Face', and stood at 'Parade-Rest', as the Major of the base smiled at the interaction, nodded to the new Marine, and continued the speech the Major had planned.

As the speech finished moments later, and the families left the stands in a rush to gather and greet their new Service Member, the young Marine lost sight of the Agent in White, and could feel as though there was something important about the interaction. A moment later, as the new Marine was greeted by his mom and family, he hugged her, broke the embrace, and with tears forming in his eyes, smiled, "Mom, I... I think that was Dad.." he said, and watched as the woman shook her head slowly, and hugged the new Marine again.

As the Agent in White loaded into the large, dark vehicle several moments later, and removed the White Fedora from their head, the face-visor from their face, and the white head-covering, tears formed in his eyes as he knew he would never see his son again, but the pride was rolling down his cheeks, as the goosebumps crawled up his arms and down his back. A second later, the phone in his pocket chimed. Reaching into his White Coat pocket, he removed the phone, pressed the green icon, and placed it to his ear, "Madam President?" he replied, reaching up to stroke his long, red braided beard as it hung from his chin.

"I, need you back here, now" Leticia demanded on the other end of the phone.

The Agent wiped his eyes and cleared his throat, "I am on my way" he replied, pulled the phone away from his head, pressed the red icon to hang up the phone, and set it next to him. Waiting for a moment, and sitting behind the dark tinted glass of the vehicle, the Agent watched as his son, the mother of his son, and the family walked by, smiling and laughing, proud of the young mans accomplishment, load into a large white vehicle, and begin to leave the base for the last time. Getting into the line of vehicles, the Agent left the base, and knew he would see his son again one day, though his son would never see him again.

Getting to the airport, the Agent in White boarded a small plane, took a seat, fastened the seatbelt across the waist, and left California towards the Capitol of the Country, Washington D.C., and the fate that awaited.

Within thirty-minutes of landing, the Agent in White arrived at the front door of the White House, saluted the Marines that stood guard outside the main doors, and entered as the doors were opened by two Agents in Yellow standing near the Marines. Walking down the halls, the Agent in White thought about the morning, and could feel a heavy weight in the building. Arriving at the Oval Office doors, and the empty desk of the Secretary, Anita, the Agent paused before entering, looking at the empty chair behind the desk, and reached up to rub the head-covering neck.

Knocking twice, and hearing the command to enter, the Agent in White twisted the doorknob to the Office, pushed the door open, and paused after the first step into the Office, and at the Guest seated on the sofa in the middle of the room.

Sitting there was Moxie, with the 'Agent in Red' attire next to her, and the Red Fedora resting on the outfit she once wore, wearing a dark-blue suit, White high heels, and her hair pulled back in a bun.

"She, is taking her old position back at the front desk.." Leticia said as she watched the Agent in White slowly enter the room, shutting the door quietly.

The Agent in White took another step inside the room, and crossed the arms in front of the heavy-breathing chest, slightly shaking the head that adorned the large-White Fedora, and cocked the head from Moxie, to the President as if to ask, 'Why?'.

"There was, ummm.." Leticia began as she slowly stood from her seated position in the large-leather chair, looked out the window to were the bodies had fallen that morning, and looked at Moxie.

"They are dead" Moxie blurted out, interrupting the President, "and, Anita, well.." she began as she pulled a small box from out of view by her feet, setting it on the coffee table, and flipping open the flaps of the box to reveal two-hands, "wont be at work today" she said, leaving the flaps open for the Agent in White to see.

The Agent removed the Fedora, and face-visor, and took a step closer to see the hands, pulling the head-covering from his head, and tossing it to the chair opposite the sofa and Moxie, "What the fuck is going on here?" he asked, reaching for the two-braids that hung from his chin, and looking from Moxie to Leticia.

For the next few moments, Leticia explained the happenings of the morning, and watched as the Agent in White stood dumbfounded at the news, taking a few more steps towards the seat he tossed his head-coverings too, pushed them aside gently, and sat, "What do we do?" he asked, looking down at the box on the table, then at the President who walked around her desk, and leaned her large-rear against the edge of the wooden desk.

"We only have a few weeks until the election" Moxie said, reaching for the box to close the flaps.

The Agent looked at his friend, "And Anita? Is she, dead?" he asked as he watched the flaps close.

Moxie shook her head, "No, she just won't ever type again, or hold her kids, or.." she said as the box was removed from the table and replaced by her feet.

The Agent held up his hand to stop her, "I get it" he replied, shaking his head and closing his eyes for a moment to mourn the tragedy that happened.

Leticia stood away from her desk, and took a step, "There's more.." she said, causing the Agent to turn his attention towards the President.

"How the fuck could there be more?" the Agent asked quickly, his tone brash and excited, "Three Leaders and the last Justice were tossed from a fucking helicopter, Anita's hands were removed, Roxie was tortured and killed.." he began as the list of devastation rolled from his mouth.

"Agents, all Agents have all begun to be assassinated.." Moxie quipped, shifting her weight as she sat, ready to stand to face the Agent in White.

The Agent in White looked at Moxie with a stunned look, then at Leticia, reached down for his Fedora and items, and began replacing on his head as he pulled the head-covering over his head.

Moxie looked at her friend with a puzzled look, "Where do you think you are going?" she asked, sounding concerned and frustrated.

The Agent in White donned the Fedora, and held the face-visor in his hand, moving it towards his face,

"He's destroying this Country, everything she has done, and is trying to do.." he said boldly with irritation and anger in his voice, gripping the face-visor tightly and feeling it bend in his hand, "he has to be stopped" he said, placing the face-visor on his face to cover the exposed flesh of eyes and bridge of his nose, and turning around sharply to leave.

"Agent.." Leticia announced quickly as she tried to stop him, her voice caring and soft.

The Agent in White paused, but didn't turn around as he slightly turned his head to acknowledge the President.

"Be safe.." Leticia said caringly, and watched as the Agent in White nodded, and walked towards the door to leave.

Moxie stood quickly, and looked at the President sternly, "That's it? That's all you have to say!?" she blurted as she motioned towards the Agent that was leaving.

Leticia scoffed softly and shook her head lightly, turning up the corner of her mouth, and walking around her desk to her seat, "What would you say to stop him?" she asked, reaching for the back of her chair, and spinning it so she could sit.

Moxie listened as the doorknob turned and the door opened, turning her attention to the sound, and shook her head sadly, "Nothing, I can say.." she said, watching her friend walk through the opened door, and closing it behind him, "be safe.." she said sadly and caringly as the door clicked shut, and he was gone.

That night, the Five-O'clock News stations aired a new segment for a new Candidate for the upcoming election, a new opposition against Leticia Gonzalez, named Shawn Mayerson. The segment was brief and to the point, and while it wasn't the Candidates voice, it showed many short video-clips of the man shooting guns, petting dogs, and encouraging Military Veterans as he laughed while wearing t-shirts, jeans, combat boots, and a cowboy hat. His smile seemed forced, as if he was a used car-salesman trying to sell the clunker that had been on the lot for far too long.

"For far too long, we have been fed lies and deceptions about what the country needs, what is best for

the people, and that we are only as weak as our weakest border" the narrator began as the segment started, *"from a President who had never served a day of Service for this Country, and sat comfy behind a desk dictating change"* the voice continued, and paused, *"and now, a new regime wants to rise, taking away our lands, our voices, and set forth a new democracy given to a weaker future of humanity"* the voice continued as it tried to strike fear to those who watched and listened, *"Under my new Presidency, we will reinstate the Prison and Jail systems, rid the homes of the Cameras of the Government, and rebuild those walls and borders to keep our Country safe"* the voice continued as the last video-clip showed the Candidate standing tall in front of the American Flag as it waved in front of a 'Green-Screen' White House image, *"Vote, Shawn Mayerson for President, or don't vote at all, Your Country deserves better"* the voice finished as the commercial segment finished, and the News Anchors sat dumbfounded and speechless.

The next morning at nine-AM, as the election day crept closer, the television shows and News agencies were interrupted by an Emergency Broadcast. With the multi-colored bars and loud-pitched tone filled the screens for a moment, alerting the viewers abruptly, the screen switched to the front doors of the White House, with two Marines standing either side of the doors, and an Agent in Yellow next to the Marines, with a wooden podium front and center, and the American, Canadian, Mexican, and Sovereign Nations flags to the left of the podium. Moments later, the Marines opened the front doors simultaneously, and saluted as the President excited the building and approached the podium as she saluted the Marines. Looking at the flags with Pride, and sadness, Leticia turned to the flags, placed her right-hand over her heart, and spoke.

"I pledge allegiance, to THESE Flags.." Leticia said boldly and with emphasis, "of the United Nations of Nations, and to the Democratic Republic of Equality, for which each of these stand, One United Nation, under the protection of the God that protects each of Us, undividable, with Liberty, and Justice for All.." she finished as she lowered her hand from her chest, turned to the cameras pointed at her, and smiled, "Today" Leticia began as the smile grew across her face, "the Peoples of this land, these Nations, are given the new choice of Truth and Understanding, as a new face of a Future has thrown their hat into the ring, to lead the next generation" she said as she paused, stepping back with her right foot and pulling her body away from the podium while still holding onto the sides of the wooden structure, looking down at her left foot, and exhaling, then pulling herself back to her composed stance, and smiling once more as the Proud Woman and President she was, "While promises are always made, and broken, it the 'Proof that's in the Pudding' that matters, and while I know I have made mistakes, and done my best for the People who have voted for me, I ask the Voters, the People, to look into their hearts, the last eight-years, and ask themselves, 'How could it have been different, and how much could it have gotten worse'?" she asked, her tone sincere as she looked straight into the camera, "What threats were made to get votes? What promises were made to get votes?" she asked, letting go of the podium and gently clasping her hands together in front of her, "How safe did our streets become, how the education system grew, the job market, 'Our' job market and economy.." she asked rhetorically, "and how it could just get better, with the demolition of the borders and crime, the unification of Nations and Peoples, and how strong our military could be for not only home, but abroad as well" she asked, her smile strong and her face unquavering, "We, can, and will, set a new standard for countries to follow as we move forward today, and after this coming election, regardless of who wins" she stated as she unclasped her hands and gripped the podium once more, "Because it is you, the Voters, who hold the power, not this public figurehead who stands, and sits, here.." she said as she gently turned and waved her left hand towards the large White building behind her, then turned back to the cameras, her smile bigger and brighter, "I am Leticia Gonzalez, President of these lands, and as always, here for YOU!" she demanded as she pointed at the camera for a moment, lowered her hand, turned slowly towards the doors of the White House, and disappeared into the building as the two Marines held the doors open for a moment as they saluted the Powerful Woman, and let the doors shut behind her.

Chapter 15

Every Country has power struggles from at least two forms of Government that want to inflict their views and control, and one is usually for the people it wants to represent, the other is for a aspect that many deem as controversial. This upcoming election was no different.

On one hand, there was Leticia Gonzalez, who had Risen from the Governorship of California, and fixed a broken and corrupt state of disarray, to leading the Nation and given the vast majority of its Citizens the voices they longed for, and deserved. She had brought the country back from near destruction, and given it the future and heart it had needed, and promised. With her views and beliefs, she had begun to send the country on a new trajectory that would see it, as well as its neighbors, become more than just a dream, but a land of the real Brave.

On the other hand, there was Larry, who was the wall against humanity, progression, and growth, and would do anything to stop what stood in his way of absolute power and control of the worlds currency and equality. And this time, the walls name was Shawn Mayerson.

There had already been one commercial in which President-Elect Mayerson had slandered the current administration, the direction of the Nation, and its neighbors and citizens. And while Leticia had come out and given her own statement and promises, she knew there would be more that would force the country to be divided.

Shawn Mayerson was the distant nephew of Larry Fisqual, and while there was no name association, there were several similarities that could link the two men together. Their eyes were just as dark and soulless, their hair had the same part on the side, their smiles were just as mischievous and untrustworthy, and their promises were just as empty and heartless. Shawn could have been Larry's illegitimate child, and Larry often wondered if he was the boy's father. There was a night at a reunion when Larry got extra drunk, smoked a little too much weed, and woke up in a bed, naked, next to his cousin, and could not remember a thing that had happened the night before. Several months later, he learned she was pregnant, and

Larry disappeared even deeper from his family, but would always be there to help and save his nephew.

When Shawn was fourteen, he was gifted a 'Get Outta Jail Free' card, with nothing more than a number on the back, and the words 'Fisqual Enterprises' in bold letters on the front. When Shawn was nineteen, he was pulled over for a taillight out, gave the Officer more grief and trouble than needed, and was arrested. He tried giving the card, but by then it was too late, and Shawn spent several nights in jail, where he was beaten up by his cellmate, had his ankle broken, and walked with a limp ever since. He vowed to hate cops after that day, and would stop at nothing to disband and defend every Law Enforcement Organization across America, with the secret backing and funding of his Uncle Larry.

There was ten-days left until the election, the skies were dark over Washington D.C. as the storm clouds began rolling in, the light rumble of thunder in the distance, and a flash of light in the sky every so often. Most of the flights in and out of D.C. that day were cancelled, not only due to the weather forecast, but also because of the threats and safety concerns leading up to the election.

Leticia sat at her desk listening to the rains gently hit her window with the winds pushing the rain East to West, the trees on the grounds gently swaying and twisting in the wind, and the Agents in Yellow guarding the acreage of the White House in full force. With their Organization under attack the last few weeks, they were hyper-diligent with their awareness and security.

'Knock-knock' came the rap on the Office door to Leticia's Office, as the door knob turned, and Moxie poked her blonde head through the crack, "Ma'am..?" she asked lightly, forcing a smile, "There's, another commercial" she said as she pushed the door open a little more, standing there in her black, ankle-length dress, black pumps, and her hair pulled back in a tight bun.

Leticia looked up from her desk and stack of files and papers she needed to sign before the election, glanced at Moxie, and shook her head, "How, bad is it?" she asked, removing her glasses from her face and placing them on the stack of unsigned papers.

Moxie exhaled deeply and shook her head, "Bad..." she replied with a nod, and left the Office, pulling the door closed as she returned to her own desk and tasks.

Leticia shook her head, reached up and gently pinched the bridge of her nose, and blindly opened the drawer next to her and removed the television remote out of memory, pointing it to the television, and pressing the 'Power' button. A moment later, the sounds of the commercial could be heard, and Leticia gave it her full attention.

"The Country is not what we were promised.." the familiar voice of Shawn Mayerson began in a smooth, callous tone as the man was at a gun range, shooting clay pigeons, and laughing, "with the illegal Mexicans overrunning our southern borders, flooding our Nation with their drugs, prostitution, and gangster ways.." he added as he set down the shotgun, and picked up an AR-15, aimed it at a silhouette of a man, and opened fire, "the Liberal views of equality diminishing the Conservative views of Trust, and Humanity, allowing the 'Gays' to infect our schooling and teachings of Respect and Tradition.." he said as the commercial switched to Shawn in a classroom, with a 'Cross' on the wall, and all the children in school uniforms with their hands folded neatly on their desks, and paying attention to the book he was holding, "And the South being overrun by the gangs, drugs, and violence of those we 'gave'.." he said with emphasis on the word, "freedom and equality to" he insisted in a hateful tone to insight those watching that had his views to be angered once more, "One of the worst things we could have done in the South, was lose that war, and taking the balance away from the real Law Enforcement the Nation needed.." the voice announced as the screen flashed to a short video of Shawn holding his hand high with the Grand Master of the Southern KKK, his face beaming next to the man covered in White, with a large Red cross on his chest, and a burning tree in the background with a several empty nooses swinging from a protruding branch, "This country is lost, to a Mexican 'Female', who never knew real loss or tragedy, suffering, or having something taken from her, but hides in her Office and lashes out at the system that was geared to protect her at the Taxpayers expense.." Shawn's voice said angrily, as the next video showed him standing behind a podium with the White House behind him, obviously a green screen image, "This coming election, vote me, Shawn Mayerson as our Next President, and give this Country back the morals and standards it once had, and was promised" he said, smiling his crooked, car-salesman smile.

Leticia's mouth fell open as she dropped the remote on her desk, and began shaking her head, "Moxie!!!" she screamed loudly, reaching up to pinch the bridge of her nose again.

A moment later, the Office door opened again as Moxie walked through, leaving the door open, and placing her hands behind her back, "Yes, Ma'am?" she asked softly and sweetly.

Leticia looked up at her Secretary, dropping her hand to her lap and shaking her head, "That was fucking disgusting" she replied angrily, her brow furrowed at what she had just watched.

Moxie nodded, her face turning sadder for a moment, "It gets worse, Ma'am" she replied, took another step inside the Office, and was followed by Sundae Jones.

Sundae walked into the Office with a purpose in her step, her pink dress swaying as she walked, "There's been a travesty in Gasquet" she announced as she approached the desk quickly, placing her hands on the wooden desk, and leaning towards Leticia.

Leticia sat back and exhaled deeply, "I don't know if I can take anymore bad news" she said as she shook her head.

"There was a shooting, a Firefighter was killed.." Sundae said quickly, "Murdered, and the fucking DA released him after seventy-two hours, for 'lack of evidence'.." she said as she stood up and gave air-quotes with fingers on either side of her head.

Leticia sat in shock for a moment, thinking back to her favorite little town, and the small bar, "Make an example of the DA.." she said as her face scowled, "and of the Agents there?" she asked, placing her right hand on the desk, and tapping her fingers from pinky to thumb quickly as her irritation of the morning grew.

Sundae shook her head and scoffed, "They wanted to keep the son-of-a-bitch there, but the fucking DA.." she said, placing her hands on the desk again and leaning towards the President, "Its that fucking Larry, I tell you..." she said frustratingly as her voice became angrier, "I swear he paid that fucking DA to drop the charges and demand the release" she said as she stared at Leticia.

Leticia nodded and looked at the television again, then back at her Vice-President, "That mother fucker has been behind a lot as of late, and I think it's time he faces the wrath he's inflicting.." she said as she looked her VP in the eyes, and stopped tapping her fingers on the desk.

The NEWS agencies ran the latest Presidential Campaign video over and over, with several boasting about the new Candidate and his views a good thing for the country, and the other agencies revolting against the hate and bigotry of the Candidate. Calls flooded the Radio Stations and Broadcasts with their support, and hatred, for the Candidate, and while the Country tore itself apart over the idea's of the commercial and its Campaign, Larry sat high in his hidden Office, and smiled.

For eight-days, crime rose across the country as the NEWS agencies, depending on their political views and affiliations, flooded the country and airwaves with their own propaganda, enticing and infuriating the masses to stand their ground, and voice their opinions. Leticia watched the crime across the country, as well as Canada, and Mexico, double, as the other Candidates message and ideas were spread like a wildfire. The South, Mississippi, Alabama, and Georgia, saw kidnappings and lynching's increase based on not only the color of their skin, but their sexuality, religion, and political views. Several Voting sites were burned to the ground in each state, and a State of Emergency was broadcast Nationwide.

The morning of election day, Leticia sat at her desk, hearing the reports from Moxie and Sundae Jones, about the deaths across the Nations, the crime increase that deafened her Law Reforms, and thought of Larry sitting in his hidden bunker laughing as the world burned. She thought about the senseless violence that plagued California before she took the Governor Office, how quick she was able to turn the state around in just four years, and how that must have infuriated Larry then. This was his payback.

9 798301 198823